STEP-BY-STEP

Excel 5.0

Sue Nugus and Steve Harris

NEW·TECH

Newtech
An Imprint of Butterworth-Heinemann Ltd
Linacre House, Jordan Hill, Oxford OX2 8DP

   A member of the Reed Elsevier plc Group

OXFORD   LONDON   BOSTON
MUNICH   NEW DELHI   SINGAPORE   SYDNEY
TOKYO   TORONTO   WELLINGTON
First published 1994
© Sue Nugus and Steve Harris 1994

NOTICE
The authors and the publisher have used their best efforts to prepare this book, including the computer examples contained in it. The computer examples have all been tested. The authors and the publisher make no warranty, implicit or explicit, about the documentation. The authors and the publisher will not be liable under any circumstances for any direct or indirect damages arising from any use, direct or indirect, of the documentation or computer examples contained in this book.

TRADEMARKS/REGISTERED TRADEMARKS
Computer hardware and software brand names mentioned in this book are protected by their respective trademarks and are acknowledged.

British Library Cataloguing in Publication Data
A catalogue record for this book is available from the British Library.

ISBN 0 7506 1810 8

Typeset by TechTrans Ltd, Reading.

Printed and bound in Great Britain.

Contents

10

About This Book

Step By Step Excel For Windows 5.0 is a practical, introductory book that you can work through at your own pace. It is important to note that this is not an exhaustive text that covers all the features offered by Excel 5.0 for Windows. Instead we have selected those areas that we believe most people need to be able to use competently in order to work productively with this package.

For the most part this book concentrates on teaching you to work with the mouse as much as possible, which is the quickest way to learn any new Windows application. Excel, like most Windows applications provides shortcut key combinations for many operations and once you have worked through this book you will then be able to look for shortcuts to reduce the time it takes you to perform certain tasks.

Typographical Conventions

To help you identify different aspects of Excel 5.0 for Windows the following list shows how we have represented commands, menus, user entries etc. In addition we have referred to the application simply as 'Excel'.

*File	Open*	Bold italics have been used for menu selections.
=B1+C5	Bold text has been used where you must type something in to a document.

The *Print* button	Plain italics have been used for Buttons on toolbars and in dialogue boxes and for list names from which you must make a selection.
TAB	Key names have been repesented in small capital letters.
ALT+TAB	The plus key (+) indicates that you should hold down the first key whilst pressing the second key.
the Record Macro dialogue box	Capitalisation has been used for references to dialogue boxes and to toolbars.

ONE
Getting Ready

Key Learning Points in this Chapter

- An introduction to Excel
- New features in Excel 5
- Hardware and software requirements
- An overview of DOS
- Windows fundamentals
- Windows applications
- Installing Excel

Background to Excel

Microsoft have had a brief, but successful history. From supplying the operating system to IBM for the PC, they have become one of the most successful software companies in the world.

From that small start, they have grown and grown, not only producing the industry standard operating systems and environments such as MS-DOS and Windows, but also producing a range of applications that are difficult to fault.

Excel was one of the first applications to be released for the Windows environment by Microsoft during their expansion. Initially it competed with long-term favourites such as Lotus 1-2-3, which at the time held a massive share of the market. This meant that in its early days Excel was not as popular as its developers would have liked, offering little that was not available elsewhere, whilst being hampered by the brand-new Windows interface.

However, as Windows developed and became easier to use, Windows applications started to become more common, rapidly overtaking the older DOS-based software in terms of new sales and general popularity. The real turning point was the release of Excel 4, which provided a whole new way of working for spreadsheet users. Excel 5 has built on this firm foundation, and provides even more in the way of time saving shortcuts, powerful analysis tools, and flexible presentation techniques.

Microsoft Office

Of course Excel is not the only Microsoft application. An entire suite of complementary products is available offering a word processor, graphics, project management, interpersonal mail and many other features beside. This group of applications is known as the Microsoft Office, and can be purchased as a bundled set or as individual packages.

The great thing about all of these programs is that they work in much the same way, and so after having learnt to use Excel you'll find that you can master other products in the set in about half the time it might otherwise take.

Of course there are other benefits as well, including easy transfer of information from one application to another, automated use of the mail system through any of the applications and so on.

Other books in this "step-by-step" series have been written to show you how to make the most of Word 6 and the other Microsoft Office applications.

New Features in Excel 5.0 for Windows

Excel 5 is a substantial upgrade over Excel 4, offering a whole variety of powerful new tools and techniques. The following sections summarise some of the more important additions and changes.

Workbooks

All Excel 5 models and plans use *workbooks*. These are effectively multiple-sheet files, with each separate sheet being the equivalent of an Excel 4 worksheet, chart or macro sheet. In fact workbooks were available within Excel 4 to make the management of complex models easier; Excel 5 simply makes them obligatory.

Charting

Whilst Excel 4's charting ability was quite flexible, it was not as easy to use as some would have liked. Excel 5 features a brand-new charting engine, with extra graph types, formatting options and editing techniques.

TipWizard

A revolutionary new feature is the TipWizard. This monitors what you are doing, and if it can find a better way, or even and alternative way, of achieving the same objective it tells you.

Cell Formatting

Excel 5 now supports the formatting of individual characters within a cell, so it is possible to apply different colours, fonts, type sizes and styles as required.

Database Management

The database features have been renamed as *list management* features, a title that more accurately describes the tasks that most users will want to perform. All of the techniques for managing lists have been substantially revised from Excel 4, and are now much quicker and easier to use. For example a list can be sorted with just a single click of the mouse button.

In addition, Excel 5 has improved analysis features for working with lists or databases, including the Pivot Table. This is a flexible way of summarising and analysing data, working in a very similar way to the Lotus Improv analysis features.

Finally, Excel 5 can gain direct access to external databases, such as those created with dBase, Paradox, Foxpro, SQL Server, Oracle, and of course Microsoft Access.

OLE Support

Excel 5 now supports the OLE version 2, which means that it is able to take advantage of all the data transfer capabilities of other OLE aware applications such as Microsoft Word for Windows 6.

Macros and Application Development

The automation of repetitive tasks has always been a requirement for many users, and Excel 5 makes this easier than ever through the provision of Visual Basic, Applications Edition. This is a version of the commercial Visual Basic development language that has been fine-tuned and modified for the spreadsheet environment. It is easy to understand, easy to modify, and extremely powerful.

Users of existing Excel 4 macro systems need not worry; all excel 4 macros should continue to function in their original form. Excel 5 even has the ability to create macros in Excel 4 format if you prefer to work that way.

What You Need to Have

In order to work so hard for you, Excel has some fairly stringent hardware and software requirements. These must be met before you can install and use the software.

Minimum Hardware Requirements

Like other Windows software, Excel requires a powerful PC and plenty of storage. The following table summarises the requirements, showing both the minimum and recommended specifications:

	Minimum	Recommended
PC Processor Memory	80286 4MB	80486 at 33MHz 8MB or more
Free disk space	8MB	25MB
Floppy disk drive	3½" or 5¼" high density	3½" or 5¼" high density
Video adapter	EGA or above	VGA or above

Note that the brand names of the PC and any peripherals are largely irrelevant – any system that is compatible with the Microsoft Windows environment should be suitable.

Printers

Excel is capable of producing very high quality output, comprised of a combination of text and graphics. However, for this to print satisfactorily it will be necessary to have a high-quality laser printer or similar. The two most popular laser printer "families" are PostScript printers and HP LaserJet printers (and their compatibles).

PostScript printers tend to be the most flexible, offering a number of in-built fonts and graphical effects. They are typically equipped with 2MB of more of memory, and have their own on-board processor and so are ideally suited to Windows applications such as Excel.

HP LaserJet printers, and especially the compatibles, tend to be less expensive. Ideally they need to be equipped with at least 2MB of printer memory to allow them to print the graphics that Excel can produce.

A good compromise may be to buy a LaserJet (or compatible) printer that can later be upgraded by the addition of a PostScript cartridge. If this approach is taken then it is recommended that only a good brand-name printer is chosen (such as a true Hewlett-Packard) as this will minimise compatibility problems.

Software

In addition to the hardware requirements there is also a need to have a certain level of software installed prior to Excel.

Firstly, the operating system should be either DOS 5 or DOS 6.X. Proprietary versions from the manufacturer of the PC (such as Compaq, IBM, Toshiba) are fine as long as they are the right numeric version. You can check this by typing VER at the DOS command prompt. A message similar to the following should be produced:

```
C:\WINDOWS>ver

MS-DOS Version 5.00
```

In addition to the operating system, it is necessary to have Microsoft Windows installed. The minimum version that is required is Windows 3.1. Windows for Workgroups 3.1 or 3.11 will also work without problems, also providing mail facilities for communicating and transferring data to other users.

To check which version of Windows is installed, choose *Help*, *About Program Manager* from the main Windows desktop. Figure 1.1 shows the dialogue box that will be displayed:

This book assumes that DOS and Windows have already been installed onto the PC. If not, consult the documentation that was supplied and carefully follow the installation guidelines.

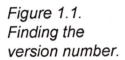

Figure 1.1.
Finding the
version number.

Version Number ————

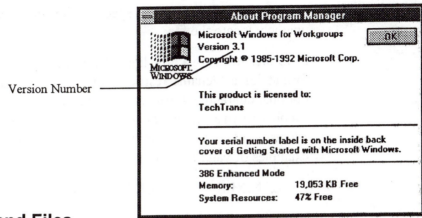

DOS, Directories and Files

In order to efficiently manage the information on your PC, it will be necessary to know a little about the operating system – DOS. This is the underlying piece of software that allows you to run programs such as Excel, but it is also responsible for ensuring that your documents and information are stored correctly. In effect it is your filing system.

DOS works on the basis of textual commands which you type in from the keyboard when you want DOS to do something. These commands bear some similarity to English; for example, COPY duplicates information, ERASE removes it and so on. Some of the most relevant commands are discussed below.

The majority of these commands relate to the storage and management of your information. This is stored in the form of separate files, groups of which can be managed in directories.

Files and Filenames

A DOS file is similar to a conventional paper-based file. It holds information in a logical order, it is referenced by name and it is stored somewhere, in this case on a disk rather than in a filing cabinet.

Files are created by your applications when you work with them. The process of creating a file is usually called Saving, whilst the process of retrieving an existing file is known as *Opening* or *Loading*. When these operations are performed, it is necessary to specify a filename – an identifier that is used to uniquely locate the file.

DOS filenames are a little limited in terms of what is allowed. The standard format for a filename restricts you to just 8 characters, with a further 3 optional characters being used by the software. The 8 character portion is simply known as the *filename*, whilst the 3 character portion is known as the *extension*. These two sections are separated by a ".". The following are examples of valid filenames:

PLAN.XLS   MYLETTER.TXT   SAMPLE.

Notice that the third example has no file extension – this is perfectly valid as the extension is optional. The extension is used to categorise the files into different types, so for example an XLS extension indicates that the file contains an Excel spreadsheet, whilst an extension of DOC signifies that the file contains a Word document.

Both the name and extension are restricted to using only certain characters, namely alphanumeric characters and some punctuation symbols. However, it is advisable to use only the following, to minimise any confusion:

Letters	A–Z
Numbers	0–9
Underscore	_

The underscore character should be used where a space is required. It is also worth remembering that upper and lower case are considered to be the same, so BUDGET.XLS is the same as Budget.xls.

The following are examples of valid and invalid filenames:

Valid	Invalid
FORECAST.XLS	SAMPLES93.DOC (Too many letters)
MEMO_JAN.DOC	NOTES**.XLS (No * allowed)
FIRST.	TEL NUMS.LST (No spaces allowed)
Clients.XLS	

Directories

All of the available files can be listed in a *directory*, which shows their names, extensions, sizes, and the date and time they were last modified. A typical directory listing may appear as follows:

```
Volume in drive C has no label
 Volume Serial Number is 1AD9-4D80
 Directory of C:\WIN

256COLOR BMP        5078 10-01-92    3:11a
AB       DLL       97584 10-01-92    3:11a
ACCESSOR GRP        6230 12-31-93    2:40p
APPLICAT GRP        5924 12-31-93    2:40p
ARCADE   BMP         630 10-01-92    3:11a
ARGYLE   BMP         630 10-01-92    3:11a
ARTGALRY INI          89 12-17-93   10:11a
BOOTLOG  TXT        2458 06-25-93   11:11a
CALC     EXE       43072 10-01-92    3:11a
CALC     HLP       18076 10-01-92    3:11a
CANYON   MID       33883 10-01-92    3:11a
CARDFILE HLP       24810 10-01-92    3:11a
```

Notice that in this example the files are sorted by their filename. If you display a list of files on your computer's disk then they may be sorted into a different order, if at all. The topic of sorting files is discussed in the DOS reference manuals.

The Directory Tree

As you can imagine, once a few files have been created, such a directory listing would become extremely long and difficult to read. To overcome this problem files can be grouped and stored in subdirectories. You can think of a subdirectory as being analogous to a drawer in a filing cabinet, with each file being the equivalent of a single document within that drawer. Unlike the filing cabinet however, subdirectories are hierarchical – that is they form a tree-like structure which is collectively known as the *directory tree*. Diagramatically the directory tree can be represented as shown below:

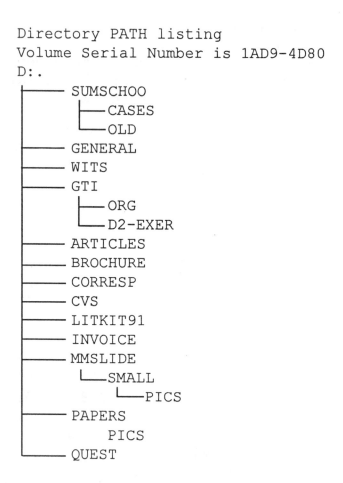

```
Directory PATH listing
Volume Serial Number is 1AD9-4D80
D:.
├─── SUMSCHOO
│       ├─CASES
│       └─OLD
├─── GENERAL
├─── WITS
├─── GTI
│       ├─ORG
│       └─D2-EXER
├─── ARTICLES
├─── BROCHURE
├─── CORRESP
├─── CVS
├─── LITKIT91
├─── INVOICE
├─── MMSLIDE
│       └─SMALL
│             └─PICS
├─── PAPERS
│          PICS
└─── QUEST
```

Notice that each subdirectory has a name, and this must obey the same rules as a standard filename. Note that it is quite possible for a subdirectory to have an extension as well as a name, although this is not usually included.

When viewing the contents of a subdirectory in the form of a directory listing, some differences will be apparent when compared with the simple directory listing shown previously.

The following is an extract from the full directory listing that corresponds to the directory tree shown above:

```
Volume in drive D has no label
 Volume Serial Number is 1AD9-4D80
 Directory of D:\DATA

 .                <DIR>        07-09-93      9:45a
 ..               <DIR>        07-09-93      9:45a
 GTI              <DIR>        07-09-93      9:46a
 ARTICLES         <DIR>        07-09-93      9:46a
 BPR              <DIR>        10-06-93      9:44a
 BROCHURE         <DIR>        07-09-93      9:46a
 CASEBOOK         <DIR>        07-09-93      9:48a
 CORRESP          <DIR>        07-09-93      9:46a
 CVS              <DIR>        07-09-93      9:46a
 DAN              <DIR>        07-09-93      9:49a
 DELPHI           <DIR>        07-09-93      9:47a
 GENERAL          <DIR>        07-09-93      9:46a
 GLOSSARY         <DIR>        08-24-93      9:41a
 IMAGES           <DIR>        07-09-93      9:47a
 INVOICE          <DIR>        07-09-93      9:46a
 LITKIT91         <DIR>        07-09-93      9:46a
 MMCONF94         <DIR>        07-26-93      4:46p
 MMSLIDE          <DIR>        07-09-93      9:46a
 PAPERS           <DIR>        07-09-93      9:47a
 QUEST            <DIR>        07-09-93      9:48a
```

Notice that the top two entries are . and .. – these are special entries that are used to move between the subdirectories. More will be seen about these entries later. Following the two special entries, the remainder of the listing consists of the names of the subdirectories. For example, the first subdirectory is called **GTI**, the second is called **ARTICLES** and so on. Notice that these correspond to the subdirectories shown in the graphical directory tree.

The first directory is known as the *root directory,*. Rather than having a name, the root directory is referenced using the "\" character. Furthermore, the root directory will be found to have no "." or ".." entries in its directory listing so it is a rather special case.

Disk Drives

Most computers are equipped with multiple disk drives, each of which is capable of storing a separate directory tree. Two types of disk drive may be encountered; floppy disk drives and hard disk drives.

Floppy disk drives allow different disks to be used on the PC, as the disk may be removed from the drive by opening the door. Hard disk drives are not removable, and are housed inside the PC. Because there is no need to make the disk accessible, hard disk drives operate at higher speeds, and are capable of storing greater amounts of information than floppy disk drives, and therefore are traditionally used as the main storage device. Floppy disks, due to their ability to be interchanged, are traditionally used for backups and for transferring information between computers.

When working with floppy disks make sure that you have read the guidelines for handling them and inserting them into the disk drives. These guidelines should have been supplied with your computer.

In order to differentiate between the different drives, alphabetic letters are used. Drive letters A and B are used to reference floppy disks, whilst drive letters C, D etc. are used to reference hard disks. Note that this scheme is used even on computers that have only a single floppy disk – A and B both refer to the same drive in this case.

Commands

DOS operates through the use of English-like commands. These are entered from the keyboard, and must be correctly spelt for them to be recognised. So that you will know when you can enter a command, DOS displays a prompt similar to the following:

```
D:\DATA\ARTICLES>
```

From this prompt you can see the current drive (D) and directory (\DATA\ARTICLES). This is the location where your command will take effect. For example, an ERASE command would erase some or all of the files in this location.

The appearance of the DOS prompt is a signal to you that the computer is waiting for you to enter a command, and the prompt will remain on screen until you do so. All of the available commands are discussed in the DOS manual that was provided with your PC, although one of the most important - Copy - is discussed in more detail below.

Copying Files

Files can be copied from one location to another using the COPY command. These locations could be different subdirectories, different drives or even different filenames within the same directory. It is up to you to specify this when you enter the command. The full *syntax* or layout of the command is:

```
COPY <Source File> <Destination File>
```

<Source File> refers to the name and location of the file to be copied, and <Destination File> tells DOS where you want to copy it to. Both source and destination can be specified as filenames, directory names, drive letters or any combination. Notice that there must be a space between the source and destination filenames.

For example, COPY FINPLAN1.XLS FINPLAN1.BAK copies the file called FINPLAN1.XLS to a new file called FINPLAN1.BAK, both of which will be in the current directory. However, COPY FINPLAN1.XLS A:\FINPLAN1.XLS copies the file to the root directory on disk A.

More information about the copy command can be found in the DOS reference manuals, but you should remember that it is not the only way to duplicate files. Windows is supplied with a utility to handle files called *File Manager*. This is discussed in the Windows reference manuals, and may be found to be easier to use for anyone already experienced with DOS.

Remember that you should regularly use File Manager or the DOS Copy command to make security backups of your files onto floppy disks, just in case the originals (usually on the hard disk) are damaged in some way.

Working with Directories

As mentioned, files are held within subdirectories on the disk. These are created and managed using three DOS commands MKDIR (or MD) to make a directory, CHDIR (or CD) to change to a different directory and RMDIR (or RD) to remove a directory.

For example, if you are currently working in a directory called DATA on the C drive (i.e. the DOS prompt shows C:\DATA>), a subdirectory called WPFILES could be created with:

```
MD WPFILES
```

If you wanted to then make the WPFILES directory current then you would use the following command:

```
CD WPFILES
```

At this stage the DOS prompt would read C:\DATA\WPFILES>. All commands issued would be executed in this directory, until you issued another CD command to move somewhere else. For example, to move back to the parent directory (C:\DATA) you would use either:

```
CD ..        or        CD \DATA
```

The WPFILES directory could then be removed with the RD command:

```
RD WPFILES
```

Note that it is *not* possible to remove a directory if it contains any files or subdirectories or if it is current (i.e. you are working in it).

Creating the STEPXL Working Directory

The files created and used in the exercises throughout this book are assumed to be stored in a directory on the hard disk called STEPXL. To create this directory :

1   Ensure you are in the root directory by typing CD \ ENTER
2   Type MD STEPXL ENTER

Running Windows

Perhaps the most important DOS command of all as far as we are concerned is the one that allows us to start Windows. This is done with the WIN command, which can be entered at any DOS prompt.

On entering the command, the screen should go blank for a few seconds and then display the Microsoft Windows Logo and copyright screen. After a few more seconds the main Windows display should appear. Obviously these timings are approximate and could vary quite substantially, especially on a slower computer system.

Windows Fundamentals

Windows provides a graphical user interface to allow you to work quickly and easily with the computer. This means that unlike DOS, commands are issued by pointing and clicking using the mouse, and information is displayed in graphical "windows".

The Desktop

The main working area is known as the *desktop*, and appears as shown in Figure 1.2. Note that the term "Desktop" refers to the entire shaded area – the section in the middle is called the Program Manager Window and is where you will be working from most of the time.

Figure 1.2.
The Windows
desktop.

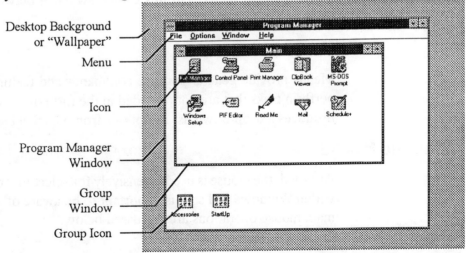

There are three main features that you can work with in Program Manager – icons, groups and menus. In addition, there are numerous other controls and features as we will see.

Icons

Icons are small images that represent individual programs or files. Activating an icon will run the program or load the data file as appropriate.

The actual image used for the icon usually gives some clue as to what the program will do. For example, a text editor may have a pen as its icon, whilst a drawing program may have a paintbrush and paint palette. There is also a short description of the icon shown beneath the image to give further information.

Groups

Groups contain icons. In many ways groups can be thought of as the Windows equivalent of a subdirectory, with the icons representing the files and programs. However, groups are not hierarchical; in other words you cannot have a group within a group.

Groups can be shown in two ways, as group icons, in which case their contents are hidden, or as visible groups, in which case the icons within the group are also visible. Groups can be switched between being visible and "iconised" using the mouse.

Menus

Menus provide general purpose commands and features that allow you to perform tasks that are not provided in the form of icons. Activating a menu produces a drop-down list of options from which a choice may be made.

Using the Mouse

As noted, the mouse is used extensively for selecting and issuing commands within Windows and so it is important to be aware of what is possible. The main mouse operations are discussed below.

Moving

The mouse position is represented on screen as a mouse cursor, usually a pointing arrow but occasionally it may be shown as some other shape such as a cross, double headed arrow, hand etc. Different shapes are used to denote different functions and behaviour.

The mouse cursor moves in synchronisation with the mouse itself. For example, moving the mouse away from you should move the cursor up the screen, whilst moving the mouse towards you moves the cursor down the screen. Similarly moving the mouse left and right moves the cursor accordingly.

As you move the mouse you may notice the cursor change shape occasionally, especially when it is positioned over the border (edge) of a group. These different shapes signify that the mouse could be used to manipulate the group if required. We will come back to this later.

Clicking

In addition to moving the mouse cursor, the mouse can be used to activate icons, groups and menu options when the cursor is positioned over them by pressing its buttons. Clicking is the process of pressing and releasing the mouse button just once, and is used to select menu choices.

By default, Windows assumes that the left mouse button will be used for this purpose. If necessary this can be changed so that the right mouse button is used instead. This is covered in the reference manuals supplied with the Windows software.

Double-clicking

Double-clicking is achieved by pressing and releasing the mouse button twice in quick succession. This is used to activate icons and groups. As with single-clicking, Windows assumes that the left mouse button will be used.

A tip worth noting is that you need to keep the mouse perfectly still when double clicking. If it is moved, Windows sees the two button presses as two separate clicks rather than one double-click. Not surprisingly some newcomers to Windows find double-clicking somewhat awkward, although with a little practice it will soon become second nature.

Right-clicking

Some programs, such as Excel, support the use of the right mouse button as a shortcut to some common operations. This is pressed and released in the same way as the left mouse button.

Dragging

Some tasks require that you move or copy information with the mouse, and this is accomplished by dragging. This means that you position the mouse cursor on the item that you want to move, press and hold the left mouse button, then drag the cursor to the required destination. Only then do you release the mouse button.

Other Mouse Operations

Some applications allow you to use the mouse in some other way. For example, Word allows a paragraph of text to be selected by *triple-clicking* the left mouse button. Excel does not use any such shortcuts, so single-clicking, double-clicking and dragging will be sufficient.

Using the Keyboard

In addition to using the mouse to issue commands, Windows allows the keyboard to be used to perform the same tasks. There are in fact two ways of using the keyboard – *hot keys* and *shortcuts*.

- A hot key is a key or combination of keys that can be pressed to simulate mouse actions.

- A shortcut is a key combination, often involving the CTRL, ALT or SHIFT keys, that duplicates the effects of several mouse operations.

Shortcut keystroke combinations often save time as they minimise the number of keystrokes or mouse clicks that are required to perform a task or series of tasks.

Identifying Hot Keys

Hot keys are recognisable on screen as they have an underline beneath the letter or character to be used. For example, the first menu option in most applications is File, with the underline signifying that F is the hot key for this option.

To use a hot key, the ALT key is pressed and held whilst the hot key character is pressed and released. This will trigger the appropriate action, as if you had clicked on the item with the mouse. However, if you want to select an option from a menu that is currently displayed, the hot key alone may be pressed.

Identifying Shortcuts

Shortcut keystrokes can be identified when a menu has been dropped-down, as they are shown alongside the appropriate menu options.

To use a shortcut key combination, press the indicated keys, remembering the CTRL, ALT and SHIFT will all have to be held down whilst other keys are pressed.

Figure 1.3 shows the File menu options available from the Windows Program Manager, together with their hotkeys and shortcuts.

Figure 1-3.
File menu
options.

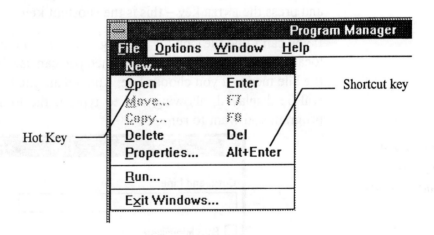

As you can see, each of the hot keys is underlined whilst the shortcut key combinations are shown to the right of the options.

Windows Applications

The different techniques that can be used may appear somewhat daunting to the novice Windows user, but this need not be so. Windows is designed to be intuitive; in other words you should be able to work out what you need to do to achieve a certain goal just by looking at the screen.

In fact a good way to learn to use Windows is to do just that – start an application (the Solitaire game is a good one to try) and use the mouse to see what happens if you click, double-click and drag. Solitaire is very similar to the card game commonly known as *patience*, and supports all of the mouse and keyboard options when you are playing the game.

However, before proceeding there are just a few fundamental operations that you need to be aware of.

Running an Application

An application can be run by double-clicking its icon. Alternatively if you can't successfully double-click yet, then single click the icon to highlight it and press the ENTER key – this is the shortcut key.

If you can't find the icon for the program you want to run, but you know the location and name of the program, then you can use the Run command under the File menu. If you choose File, Run a dialogue box similar to Figure 1.4 will be displayed, allowing you to type in the location and name of the program you want to run.

Figure 1.4.
The Run
dialogue box.

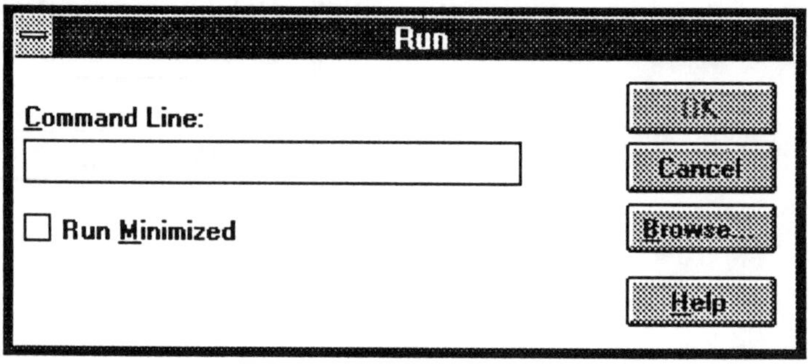

Run
Command Line:	OK
	Cancel
☐ Run Minimized	Browse...
	Help

Into the *Command Line* box you would type the drive, directory and filename of the program you want to run. For example the DOS Editor can be run by entering

C:\DOS\EDIT.COM

Closing an Application

When you have finished with an application you should close it down. Normally there will be an Exit option on the File menu that will allow you to do this, but you can also use the standard shortcut – ALT+F4.

You can also use a special feature of the program's window, known as the control button. This is situated at the very top left of the window, as shown in Figure 1.5.

Single-clicking the control button produces a special menu, known as the control menu. One of the options on the control menu is Close, which will shut down the current application. In fact double-clicking the control menu also has the same effect.

*Figure 1.5.
The Control
button.*

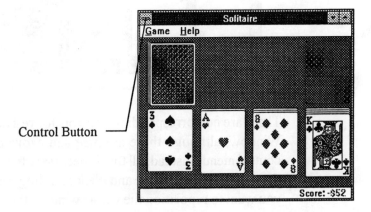

Control Button

Minimising, Maximising and Restoring

When a program is running, its on-screen window can be shown in one of three different states; *Minimised, Maximised* or *Restored.*

- A minimised window is shown as an icon at the bottom left of the desktop area.

- A maximised window will completely fill the desktop area.

- A restored window is in a flexible condition, being neither maximised nor minimised. Instead, the position and size of the window can be adjusted using the mouse

The controls that are used to minimise and maximise a window are shown in Figure 1.6.

Figure 1.6.
Minimise and
Maximise buttons.

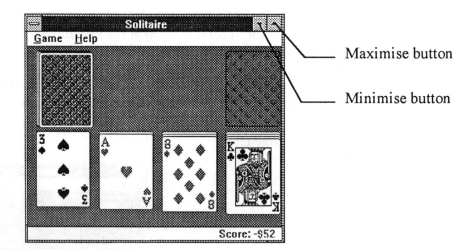

Maximise button

Minimise button

There are no corresponding controls for resizing or repositioning a restored Window, although there are *Size* and *Move* options available through the control menu. Instead, all that is necessary to resize the window is to position the cursor over its edge and click and drag that edge to its new position. If you want to reposition the whole window then move the cursor onto the title bar and click and drag to move it.

As you move or resize the window you will see a transparent grey outline whilst you are dragging; the content of the window will be redrawn when you release the mouse button.

Having maximised a window, the maximise button will change to show a double-headed arrow. This is the restore button and will appear as shown in Figure 1.7.

Figure 1.7.
The Restore button.

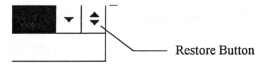

Restore Button

If the desktop is completely filled by a maximised application then all other windows will be hidden. If you wanted to access one of these hidden applications then you would need to use one of the following techniques.

The Task List

Once you have several applications running it may become confusing as to exactly what has been closed and what has not. The task list will show you exactly what is currently active, and will allow you to control each of the applications.

The task list is displayed when you press ALT+ESC, or when you choose the Switch To option from a control menu. The task list appears as shown in Figure 1.8.

Figure 1.8.
The Task List.

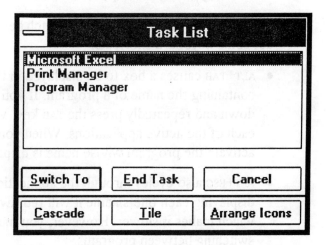

Three programs are listed in this example, Microsoft Excel, Print Manager and Program Manager (the one that contains your icons). The one at the top of the list, Excel, is the one that we are currently working with.

The buttons beneath the list allow you to manage the programs as follows:

- **Switch To** will activate the highlighted program, and remove the task list from the screen. Note that activating (which takes you into an existing program), is not the same as running (which executes another copy of that program).

- **End Task** is the same as closing the application from the control menu or with a File, Exit command.

- **Cancel** causes the task list to be removed from the screen, without taking any other action at all.

- **Cascade** and **Tile** cause Windows to position each of the programs so that some or all of each of their windows is visible.

- **Arrange Icons** moves all of the minimised programs to the bottom of the screen, positioning their icons at equal intervals.

Switching Between Applications

In addition to using the task list to switch between applications, you can also use some keyboard shortcuts.

- ALT+TAB causes a box to be displayed in the centre of the screen containing the name of a program. If you continue to hold the ALT key down and repeatedly press the TAB key, Windows will cycle through each of the active applications. When you release the TAB key you will activate the program whose name is displayed.

- ALT+ESC also cycles through the applications, although rather than just displaying each one's name it will redraw the whole of its display, which makes it slower. However, you may find this a clearer way of switching between programs.

For example, assuming you are currently working with Excel, and you also have Paintbrush and Program Manager running, pressing ALT+TAB will display the name of the previous application you used, Paintbrush:

 Paintbrush - (Untitled)

Holding the ALT key down and pressing TAB again displays the name of the next program in the sequence, in this case Program Manager:

 Program Manager

If TAB is pressed a third time with the ALT key held down, then the box will show the details for Excel:

 Microsoft Excel

Remember that to obtain this sequence the ALT key must be held down continually, only being released when the box shows the name of the program you want to switch to.

In addition to using the keyboard, the mouse can also be used to activate an application providing you can see any part of its window on screen. Simply clicking on something that is in the background will bring it forwards and make it completely visible.

Closing Windows

When you have finished working with your applications, it is very important to shut Windows down before you switch the PC off. Failure to observe this simple precaution could lead to serious problems later on.

The way to shut Windows down is to switch to the Program Manager using any of the previous techniques, and choose File, Exit or choose the Close option from its control menu. You will be prompted to confirm that you wish to exit Windows with the dialogue box shown in Figure 1.9.

Figure 1.9.
Exiting Windows.

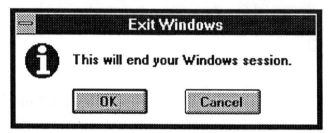

On clicking the OK button, or pressing ENTER, you will be returned to the DOS prompt. Only at this stage should you switch the PC off.

Installing Excel

Before you can go ahead and use Excel, you need to ensure that it is installed onto your computer. It may be that the software was pre-installed onto your system, which means that it should be ready to run and you can skip onto Chapter Two to learn how to use it.

However, if this is not the case (if you bought the program yourself, for example), then you need to follow the remainder of this chapter in order to get the software onto the PC.

Backing up the Disks

The first stage of installation is to make a security backup of the original disks. You need to do this just in case something happens to the disks now or in the future.

The easiest way to make a backup of the disks is to use the DOS DISKCOPY command as follows:

- Make sure that you have as many blank, formatted disks as you have original disks. Usually there are 9 or more separate disks, depending on whether you have 3½" or 5¼" disks. Your blank disks must be the same size and capacity as the originals.

- Make sure that your original disks are write protected. See your DOS and PC manuals for further information.

- Ensure that your computer is ready for you to issue commands, i.e. it is at the DOS prompt.

- Place the first of the original disks in the drive.

- If you have two identical floppy disk drives, place the first blank disk into the second drive.

- Issue the DISKCOPY command

  `DISKCOPY A: A:` or `DISKCOPY B: B:` if using a single drive

  `DISKCOPY A: B:` if using two drives (NOTE: Drive A must hold the original and Drive B must hold the blank disk)

- Follow any on-screen prompts, changing disks when necessary with a single-drive system.

- When the process has finished you will be asked if you want to copy another disk. Respond by typing Y, then repeat the above steps for the remaining disks.

- Remember to label each of the disks as they are copied so that you can identify them when they are used to install the software.

Having made your backups they should now be used for the remainder of the installation process, and your original disks stored somewhere safe.

The Installation Process

Your are now ready to install the software, so take the first of your backed-up disks and place it into the floppy drive. Start Windows, then choose the File, Run command from Program Manager.

When prompted for the command line, type in A:\SETUP if using drive A for the floppies, or B:\SETUP if using drive B. This tells Windows to run the setup program on the floppy disk. If it reports an error then make sure that you have the correct disk inserted into the drive and that the drive door is correctly closed.

As setup runs it prompts you for information. For example, the first time it is used it will ask for your name and company name so that the software can be registered to you. It will also ask you to specify what type of installation you want – Typical, Custom/Complete or Laptop.

"Typical" is likely to be the most appropriate as it ensures that all key features are installed for you. However, if you have plenty of free disk space, the "Complete/Custom" option is best as it guarantees that every feature is installed for you. The "Laptop" installation is useful only if you have limited free disk space, as it requires the smallest amount of the three techniques.

As you proceed through the Setup program you will be prompted to change disks, and may be asked for further information. If you are unsure of exactly what is required then consult the Excel documentation.

Having been successfully installed, Excel may require you to restart Windows, and may need you to reboot the PC. It will tell you on-screen exactly what you must do, and it is important to follow the instructions provided.

The Excel Group

Once installed onto your PC, the Excel icons are placed into a separate group within Program Manager. The icons within the group are shown in Figure 1.10.

Figure 1.10.
The Excel group.

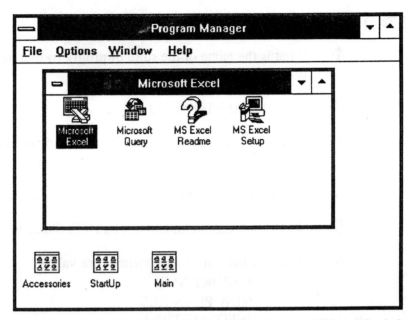

These icons are used to run Excel and its associated utilities. The leftmost one, with the title Microsoft Excel, runs the Excel program itself, whilst the second one launches a utility called Microsoft Query, for use in conjunction with external databases and lists. The question-mark icon will display the "readme" file which contains addenda and updates to the printed documentation, plus any late-breaking news about the Excel software. The final icon, Excel Setup allows you to reconfigure the software at a later date.

Summary

Excel is one of the most flexible and powerful spreadsheets available for the Windows environment. It has proven to be one of the most popular applications of the last five years, and is part of a complete range of applications that cater for all business needs.

All Excel commands can be selected using the mouse, keyboard, or a combination of both. This makes it easy for novices and experienced users alike.

Similarly the process of installing Excel onto the PC is very straightforward and should present no problems.

Self Test

1   What is the name of the suite of programs that includes Microsoft Excel, Word and Powerpoint?

2   What does the TipWizard do?

3   How much memory is needed in the PC to run Excel, and how much more is recommended?

4   Which versions of DOS and Windows are required to run Excel?

5   What is the maximum length of a DOS filename?

6   Which of the following filenames are valid?
        REPORT.XLS
        NEW PLAN.XLS
        INFORMATION

7   How do you start Windows?

8   What is an icon?

9   How do you run an application from within Windows?

10 Suggest two ways of switching between applications in Windows.

TWO
Starting Off

Key Learning Points In this Chapter

- Loading Excel 5.0
- Understanding the Excel workplace
- Toolbars
- Rulers
- Display options

Loading Excel 5.0

If you have just installed Excel by following the instructions in Chapter One you will have been asked to rerun Windows at the end of the Setup procedure.

If Excel is already on your computer and you are beginning to use the book from this point you must start-up Windows and look for the Excel icon. This may be on the opening screen when Windows is loaded as shown in Figure 2.1 or you might have to open a group icon such as Applications or Microsoft Office in order to see the Excel icon.

Figure 2.1.
The Windows
Desktop

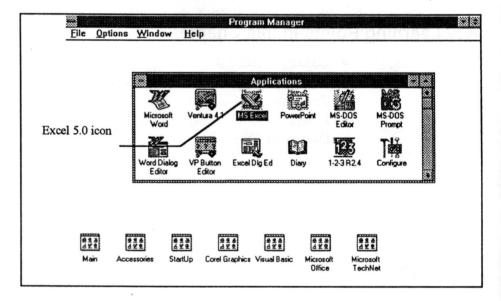

To load Excel, position the mouse over the Excel icon and double click the left mouse button. The length of time it takes to load will vary from computer to computer, but when loading is complete the screen will appear as shown in Figure 2.2.

Figure 2.2.
Opening Excel
Screen

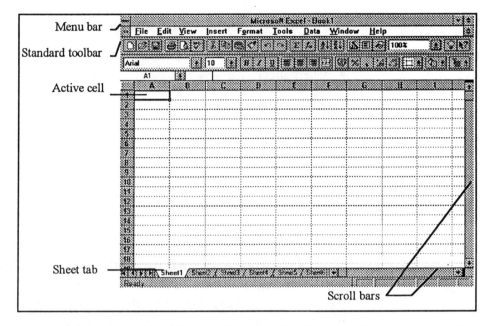

Note: *The book assumes that at this point Excel has not been customised in any way. If your system has been installed with customised toolbars the screen may not look the same. It would be preferable to re-install Excel without customisation for the purposes of working with this book.*

The Main Excel Window

Workbooks

When Excel is loaded a new, blank *workbook* is displayed as shown in Figure 2.2. This workbook is called BOOK1 and consists of 16 blank *worksheets*. Each worksheet's name appears on a tab at the bottom of the workbook. You will be able to customise the name of these worksheets as you use them, but at this stage they are labelled *Sheet 1* through *Sheet 16*. Sheets can be moved or copied between workbooks, and you can reorganise sheets within a workbook. In addition you can have several workbooks open at the same time, each in its own window.

Tip: *Think of a workbook as a ring binder file in which you place all the information, data, formulae etc. pertaining to a particular task or project.*

In addition to worksheets, a workbook can contain any combination of the following:

- Chart sheet

- Visual Basic module

- Dialogue

- Microsoft Excel 4.0 macro sheet

- Microsoft Excel 4.0 International macro sheet

Worksheets

Most of the work you do will use worksheets. As you can see in Figure 2.2 a worksheet is a grid of rows and columns, forming a series of *cells*. Each cell has a unique address. For example, the cell where column C and row 8 intersect is referred to as cell C8. You use cell references when you create formulae or reference cells in command instructions.

The *active* cell is the one into which data will be placed when you start typing. You can determine the active cell by the bold border it has around it. When you open a new workbook this will be cell A1 on sheet1.

To change the active cell you can either use the arrow keys to move one cell at a time to the left, right, up or down, or you can use the mouse to move the pointer into the required cell and then click once on the left mouse button.

Scroll Bars

To the right and the bottom right of the screen there are scroll bars which allow you to scroll up and down and left and right around the active window.

Click on the down arrow in the vertical scroll bar which will scroll the worksheet down by one row.

Status Bar

At the bottom of the screen are the horizontal scroll bar and the status bar which display information about the current document or the task you are working on. The exact information displayed will vary according to what you are doing. When you open a new workbook there are indicators to the right of the status bar that are highlighted if THE CAPS LOCK key, NUM LOCK key or SCROLL LOCK key is activated.

Toolbars

As in all Windows applications the toolbars allow quick access to commonly used commands. On starting Excel the Standard and Formatting toolbars are displayed.

Move the pointer over one of the toolbar buttons and notice the name is displayed in a small box below the selected button. This is called a *ToolTip*. A brief description of what the button does is displayed at the bottom of the screen. You can switch ToolTips on or off by checking the *Show ToolTips* box in the Toolbars dialogue box which is accessed by selecting *View | Toolbars*.

Position the pointer anywhere on the toolbar and press the right mouse button. This lists the more commonly required toolbars with a tick alongside those that are currently displayed. The current settings can be seen in Figure 2.3. In addition to these toolbars there are five more - Query, Pivot, Tip Wizard, Stop Recording and Full Screen. These may be seen on selecting *View | Toolbars* or by selecting *Toolbars* from the list in Figure 2.3.

1   Click on the Formatting option to clear the tick and the Formatting toolbar is no longer displayed.

2   With the pointer still in the toolbar area, press the right mouse button and click on the Formatting option again to redisplay the toolbar.

Figure 2.3.
Available toolbars

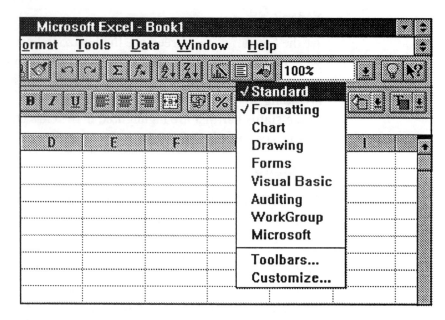

Selecting *Toolbars* from the menu displays the Toolbar dialogue box. This provides options to enlarge toolbar buttons, to add colour to buttons and to hide the ToolTips. New toolbars can be created and buttons added or removed from existing toolbars by selecting *Customize*.

Exercise

1   Display all the available toolbars.

2   Hide all but the Standard and Formatting toolbars.

The default position for the Standard and Formatting toolbars is immediately below the menu bar. As you will have seen when performing the exercise, other toolbars are displayed on different parts of the screen. By default the toolbars are *anchored* in these positions. Any toolbar can be *floated* in order that it can be moved around the screen to the required position.

1   Position the pointer on a blank part of the toolbar between buttons.

2   Hold down the SHIFT key and double-click.

3   Move the toolbar around the screen by dragging the title bar.

4   Resize the Toolbar by dragging the edge or corner.

5   Double-click the toolbar title bar to anchor it.

Exercise

1   Display the Drawing toolbar.

2   Make it a floating toolbar and resize it to be positioned horizontally at the top of the page, immediately below the Formatting toolbar.

3   Re-anchor the toolbar.

4   Hide the toolbar.

The function of various toolbar buttons will be described as they are used throughout the book.

Getting Help

Excel provides an extensive on-line help system which can be accessed in two different ways.

Help Menu

Selecting *Help* produces the list of options shown in Figure 2.4. These options enable you to access help from different entry points.

Figure 2.4
Help menu options.

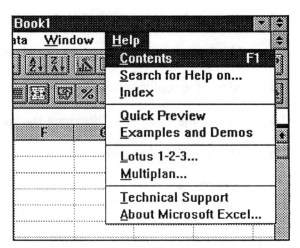

The following is a brief summary of each help menu option:

Contents
: Displays the main table of contents for the on-line help system. This falls into five broad categories, namely: Using Microsoft Excel, Examples and Demos, Reference Information, Programming with Visual Basic and Technical support.

Search for Help on
: You can select a topic on which you require help.

Index
: Displays an alphabetic index of everything in the on-line help system.

Quick Preview
: Provides a rolling tutorial of Excel features. (This is automatically presented to you when Excel is first run after installation).

Examples and Demos
: Allows you to select sample files that demonstrate in tutorial fashion how to perform selected tasks.

Lotus 1-2-3
: If you are converting to Excel from Lotus 1-2-3 this gives you specific help.

Multiplan
: Multiplan is an earlier Microsoft spreadsheet and this displays a dialogue box to help you if you are converting from this system.

THREE
Creating your First Plan

Key Learning Points in this Chapter

- Entering text and data
- Editing cells
- Creating formulae
- Summing data
- Copying formulae
- Saving Files

Introduction

In this chapter you will learn how to enter text, data and formulae into a worksheet to produce a simple business plan. You will save your file and perform some basic editing.

The worksheet that you create is a regional quarterly sales forecast for the London branch of Trendy Toys. This model will be further developed throughout the book as you learn new Excel features.

Entering Heading Text

A model heading and month names will initially be entered.

1   Click in cell A1 to ensure it is the active cell.

2   Type **TRENDY TOYS - London Branch** and press ENTER.

Note: You type the text into the Formula Bar at the top of the screen and only when you press ENTER does it appear in the active cell.

Although the text appears to extend across several columns, it is actually only stored in cell A1. As you will not be putting anything in the adjacent cells it is not necessary to widen the column. To make the heading stand out the font will be enlarged to 14 point and the words displayed in bold italic.

1   Ensure A1 is still the active cell.

2   Click on the arrow to the right of the font size box |10   ⊕| and select 14.

3   Click on the *Bold* button | B | and on the *Italic* button | *I* |.

4   Click in cell A2.

5   Type **Quarterly Sales Forecast** and press ENTER.

6   Enlarge the font to 12 point by clicking on the arrow to the right of the font size box and selecting 12.

7   Click in cell B4.

8   Type **January** and press ENTER.

9   Click the *Bold* button and the *Align Right* buttons ▦ .

It is not necessary to type in the other month names as the *AutoFill* feature can be used to extend the month names as required.

10   Click in cell B4 to ensure it is the active cell.

11   Position the mouse pointer on the small square at the bottom right of the cell border which is referred to as the *Fill Handle*. The mouse pointer will change shape to a small cross.

12   Click and drag the *Fill Handle* across to cell E4. The range is bordered by a dotted line.

13   Release the mouse button and February, March and April and automatically inserted, formatted in the same way as January in bold with right alignment. Figure 3.1 shows the model so far.

*Figure 3.1.
Model Headings
and Month
Names.*

	A	B	C	D	E
1	TRENDY TOYS - London Branch				
2	Quarterly Sales Forecast				
3					
4		January	February	March	April

AutoFill is a very flexible feature which you will use in many different circumstances. It works on the basis of extending a *series*, which in the above example is a series of month names. You could also have entered a day of the week and *AutoFill* would extend this from the first day you entered, repeating days after a week is complete. Furthermore you could enter **QTR 1** into a cell and then drag the *Fill Handle* any number of consecutive cells and Excel will fill out QTR 2, QTR 3, QTR 4 and then QTR 1, QTR 2 etc. to the end of the selected range. If you enter a series of text or data regularly into a worksheet you can customise *AutoFill* to include your own series. To do this you select **Tools | Options** and the *Custom Lists* tab.

You will use *AutoFill* later in this chapter to copy a formula that you enter into a cell, to other cells.

Trendy Toys have five categories of toys, the names of which are to be entered commencing in cell A5.

16   Click in cell A5.

17   Type **Baby & Toddler** and press the down arrow (¢)

18   Repeat the procedure for the following toy categories
    Educational
    Dolls
    Models
    Garden

Correcting Typographical Errors

If you make a typing mistake while entering anything into a cell, the BACKSPACE key will delete the character to the left of the insertion point.

If you notice a mistake when you are on a different cell, click on the cell to be corrected and then click on the edit line at the top of the screen to show the insertion point. Use the arrow keys to move to the incorrect entry. You can insert characters by typing at the insertion point and can delete the character to the right of the insertion point by pressing the DEL key.

To undo an action, including typographical errors, Excel provides the Undo feature, which is either accessed by clicking on the *Undo* button on the toolbar (↰) or through *Edit | Undo*. This will allow you to undo your last action most of the time. The menu option gives you an idea as to what the last action was. For example, if you entered a number incorrectly, under the *Edit* menu, you would find: *Undo Entry*.

Tip: *Excel allows you to edit the contents of a cell in the cell itself rather than on the Formula Bar. To do this either double-click on the cell to be edited or click once and then press F2. The insertion point will be displayed in the cell to the right of the current entry.*

Widening Columns with AutoFit

The first two categories have flowed over into column B and as you will want to enter data into these cells, column A should be widened to accommodate the additional text.

17 Select cells A5 through A9 by clicking in cell A5 and dragging down to include cell A9. Figure 3.2 shows how this selection appears on the screen. Notice how the cell border now encompasses the selected range.

Figure 3.2.
Selected range
of cells

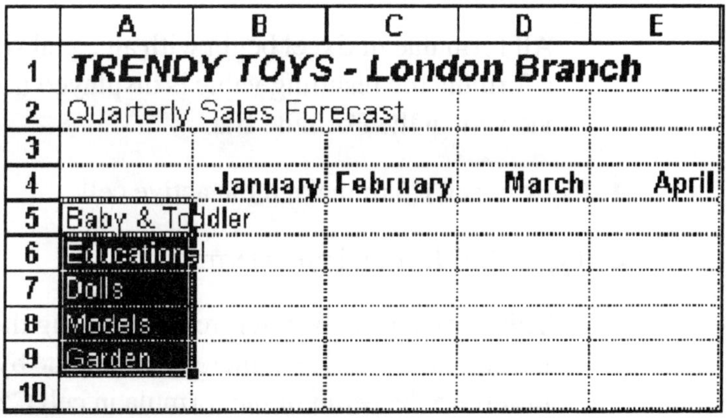

	A	B	C	D	E
1	*TRENDY TOYS - London Branch*				
2	Quarterly Sales Forecast				
3					
4		January	February	March	April
5	Baby & Toddler				
6	Educational				
7	Dolls				
8	Models				
9	Garden				
10					

18 Select *Format | Column | AutoFit Selection*

19 The column is widened to accommodate the widest entry in the selection.

Note: *Be sure not to include cell A1 in the range as this will cause column A to be as wide as the title in cell A1.*

Exercise

1 Type the heading **Total Monthly Sales** into cell A10.

2 Use the AutoFit command to widen the column appropriately.

Entering Data and Formulae

Type the following data into column B of the worksheet using ENTER and the arrow keys to move from cell to cell.

	January
Baby & Toddler	2500
Educational	2100
Dolls	3000
Models	1200
Garden	1800

The numbers are automatically right aligned in the cells.

The London branch of Trendy Toys are assuming a 1% growth per month for all product categories and so a formula is required in column C to reflect this.

All formulae in Excel begin with an equal sign (=). When you have entered a formula the resulting value is displayed in the cell and the formula can be viewed on the Formula Bar.

1 Click in cell C5 to make it the active cell.

2 Type **=B5*1.01** and press ENTER.

This formula can be interpreted as taking the current value in cell B5 and multiply it by 1.01, i.e. increase the value by 1%. If you change the value in cell B5 the result of the formula in cell C5 will automatically change.

If you made a mistake whilst entering the formula, the same editing rules that apply to editing text entries apply here. You can either select the cell and edit the contents on the Formula Bar, or you can double-click or click and press F2 to edit the contents in the cell itself.

Arithmetic Operands

Excel recognises the following arithmetic operands:

+   addition

-       subtraction

*   multiplication

/   division

^   exponentiation

%   percent when placed after a number

Order of Calculation

The formula used so far in this plan is a very simple one, but as you begin to create more complex formulae it is important to know the order in which Excel performs the calculation.

1	%	percent
2	^	exponentiation
3	* and /	multiplication and division
4	+ and -	addition and subtraction
5	&	joining text

From the above table you can see that multiplication is evaluated before addition. Therefore the formula:

$$=2+6*5$$

produces a result of 32 because 6 is multiplied by 5 first and then 2 is added. If you want a result of 40, i.e. 6 to be added to 2 and the resulting 8 to be multiplied by 5, the following is required:

$$=(2+6)*5$$

Parentheses group expressions within a formula, and any expression within parentheses is evaluated before all arithmetic operators. If you have multiple parentheses the innermost ones are evaluated first.

Copying Formulae

As this growth rate is to be the same for all products and is to compound at 1% for March and April the formula can be copied.

1   Click on cell C5 to ensure it is the active cell.

2   Position the mouse pointer on *Fill Handle* and when it changes to a small cross, click and drag down to cover the range C5:C9.

3   Release the mouse button and the formulae are inserted and the calculations performed.

4   With the range C5:C9 still highlighted, position the mouse pointer again on the *Fill Handle*, click and drag to select the range C5:E9.

5   Release the mouse button and the remaining cells are calculated.

6   Click away from the highlighted area to deselect it.

Figure 3.3 shows the current worksheet.

Figure 3.3. Worksheet with data and formulae.

	A	B	C	D	E
1	*TRENDY TOYS - London Branch*				
2	Quarterly Sales Forecast				
3					
4		January	February	March	April
5	Baby & Toddler	2500	2525	2550.25	2575.753
6	Educational	2100	2121	2142.21	2163.632
7	Dolls	3000	3030	3060.3	3090.903
8	Models	1200	1212	1224.12	1236.361
9	Garden	1800	1818	1836.18	1854.542

If you click on, for example, cell D8 you will notice that the Formula Bar reads =C8*1.01. When you copy a formula in Excel the relative relationships between cell references are always retained. You can think of this formula as being *"take what you have in the previous cell and increase it by 1%"*. There are occasions when this relative relationship is not required which is explained in Chapter Four.

Using AutoSum to Calculate Totals

Totals are required for each month and for each product category. The formula required in cell B10 is the sum of the values in the range B5 through B9.

1   Click in cell B10 to make it the active cell.

2   Select the range B5:B10 by clicking in cell B10 and dragging up to cell B5.

         Note: *Be sure to click in the cell and not on the Fill Handle when simply selecting cells.*

3   Click on the AutoSum button $\boxed{\Sigma}$ on the Standard toolbar.

4   The value 10600 is displayed in cell B10 and the Formula Bar reads =SUM(B5:B9).

         AutoSum uses the SUM *function* to total the values in the selected range. Functions are covered in more detail in Chapter 9.

         This formula can be copied for the other months by *extending the series* in the same way that the month names were extended and the growth rate formulae were copied.

1   Click on cell B10 to ensure it is the active cell.

2   Position the mouse pointer on the fill handle.

3   When it changes to a small cross, click and drag the cell border across to cell E10 and release the mouse button.

         The formula has been repeated for the other months. If you click on cell D10 you will notice that the Formula Bar reads =SUM(D5:D9).

Exercise

1   Add a column after April with a heading of Quarterly Total.

2   Increase the column width using the *AutoFit* button.

3   Use *AutoSum* to calculate the total for the first product category.

4   Copy the formula for the remaining products.

When you have completed the above exercise, the plan will appear as shown in Figure 3.4.

Figure 3.4.
Plan with
Formulae and
Totals

	A	B	C	D	E	F
1	*TRENDY TOYS - London Branch*					
2	Quarterly Sales Forecast					
3						
4		January	February	March	April	Quarterly Total
5	Baby & Toddler	2500	2525	2550.25	2575.753	10151.003
6	Educational	2100	2121	2142.21	2163.632	8526.842
7	Dolls	3000	3030	3060.3	3090.903	12181.203
8	Models	1200	1212	1224.12	1236.361	4872.481
9	Garden	1800	1818	1836.18	1854.542	7308.722
10	Total Monthly Sales	10600	10706	10813.06	10921.191	43040.251

Saving Files

As with any work on a computer it is important to regularly save because at this stage your plan is only being stored in the computer's memory, as opposed to the disk, and if the power were to fail it would be lost.

There are two ways to access the Save dialogue box by selecting *File | Save* or by clicking on the disk icon, ▣ on the Standard toolbar. Figure 3.5 shows the Save dialogue box. The default filename supplied by Excel of BOOK1.XLS may be displayed in the File Name box and this can be overwritten with your own filename.

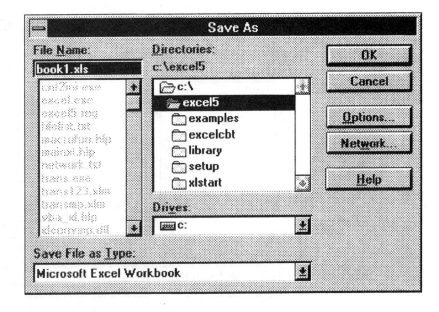

Figure 3.5.
The Save
Dialogue Box

On starting Excel the default drive is the drive Excel was installed on. This will usually be drive C on a standalone PC, but if you are working on a network it may be a different drive letter. The default directory is *excel5* which is shown under the *Directories* part of the dialogue box. At the beginning of this book you were asked to create a directory on your hard disk called STEPXL into which your work will be saved. To change to this directory:

1 Double click on C:\ in the directories section to return to the root directory.

2 Use the scroll bar to display STEPXL.

3 When this is on the screen position the mouse pointer over it and double click.

Figure 3.6 shows how the dialogue box now appears.

Figure 3.6.
Save Dialogue
Box Showing
Required
Directory

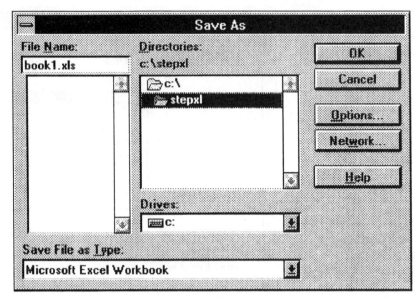

There are no files in this directory yet, and the insertion point is flashing under File Name.

4   Type TRENDY_1.

5   To complete the save either press ENTER or click once on *OK*.

If you continue working with this file and want to save it again you can click on the *Save* button on the Standard toolbar and the file will be updated using the same name. If you want to save the file with a different name you must select *File | Save As* which produces a dialogue box identical to the Save dialogue box, but you can type in a different name for the file. If the file you choose already exists you will be asked if you want to overwrite it or cancel the operation.

Keeping Backups

In the Save and Save As dialogue boxes there is an *Options* button which access the dialogue box shown in Figure 3.7.

Figure 3.7.
Save Options
Dialogue Box

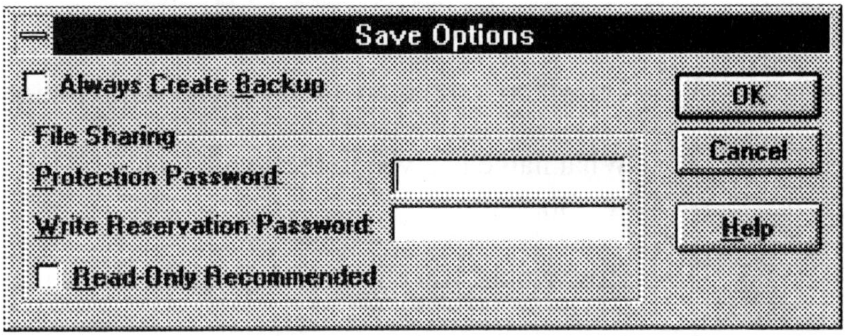

There is an option here to *Always Create Backup* which, if checked, will mean that the previous version of your file will always be retained with a .BAK file extension. Although this can be useful it is important to bear in mind that this will slow down the Save procedure with large files and each file requires approximately double the amount of disk space in order to accommodate the backup files.

File Protection

Other options in this dialogue box are concerned with file security. You can choose to protect the file with a password which has to be correctly entered before the file can be opened. Alternatively, you can choose to put a *write reservation password* on the file which means that the file can be opened and manipulated, but cannot be saved using the same name unless the password is entered.

Summary

This chapter has provided the foundation for model development in Excel which will be developed and enhanced in subsequent chapters. The use of the *extend series* feature to quickly insert month names and to copy formulae and the introduction to *AutoSum* has enabled you to produce a meaningful sales forecast plan with minimal keystrokes. In the next chapter you will learn how to improve the appearance of your plan for more professional output.

Self Test

1   On which toolbar are the *Bold* and *Italic* buttons located?

2   What name is given to the small square on the bottom right corner of the cell border?

3   How would you enter the days of the week in adjacent cells across a row?

4   How can you edit the contents of a cell from within the cell?

5   What is the effect of applying the *AutoFit* command to a range of cells.

6   What is the first character of any formula?

7   What results would the following formulae return?
         =8-2/3
         =(8-2)/3
         =8-(2/3)
         =((8-2)/3)

8   What is meant by a *relative relationship* in the context of copying a formula from one cell to another?

9   How do you total the values in a range of cells?

10   How do you update a file on disk after you have made some changes to it?

FOUR
Taking More Control

Key Learning Points in this Chapter

- Formatting cells
- Changing column widths
- Applying shading and borders
- Using AutoFormat

Introduction

The sales forecast developed in Chapter Three has given you the basic skills required to begin working productively with Excel. However, the appearance of business plans, both on screen and on paper, is important. This chapter takes the model for Trendy Toys and improves the overall appearance using some of Excel's formatting commands.

Formatting Numeric Cells

When you enter values and formulae into Excel the numbers and the results of formulae are displayed in what is referred to as *General* format. Excel calculates to 15 significant decimal places and the default column width is nine characters. Therefore you will see as many decimal places as will fit in this column width. Of course, you can change the column width to see more decimal places. With *integers* (whole numbers) Excel will display a series of hash signs (#) if the number is too big to fit in the cell. This means a numeric overflow has occurred and widening the column will allow the value to be displayed.

In most cases you will want the values in the plan to be displayed with zero, one or two decimal places, and you might want to include currency symbols on certain cells. You can change the way values are displayed by *formatting* them. It is, however, important to note that formatting cells does not change the actual contents. For example, if the result of a formula was 34.76543 and you formatted this cell to two decimal places you would see the value 34.77 displayed. But, any other cell that referenced this one would use the value 34.76543 in its calculation. If you really want to change the contents of a cell so that the value has a specified number of decimal places you must use the ROUND function. This is discussed in Chapter 9.

TRENDY_1.XLS will be further developed in this chapter so you should open it before proceeding.

1   Select *File | Open* or click on the *Open* button 🗁.

2   Ensure you are in the STEPXL directory.

3   Click on TRENDY_1.XLS and then click *OK*.

Save the file with a different name.

4   Select *File | Save As*

5   In the *Name Box* type **TRENDY_2** and click *OK*.

Figure 4.1 shows how the plan currently appears.

*Figure 4.1.
Plan before
formatting.*

The sheet box

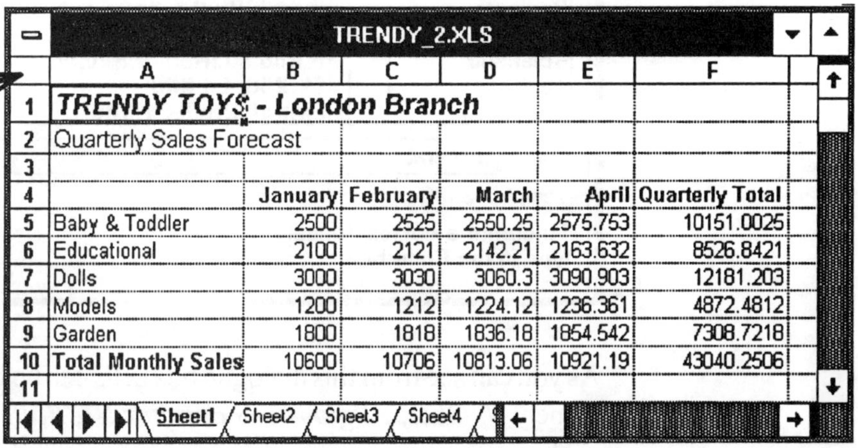

	A	B	C	D	E	F
1	TRENDY TOYS - London Branch					
2	Quarterly Sales Forecast					
3						
4		January	February	March	April	Quarterly Total
5	Baby & Toddler	2500	2525	2550.25	2575.753	10151.0025
6	Educational	2100	2121	2142.21	2163.632	8526.8421
7	Dolls	3000	3030	3060.3	3090.903	12181.203
8	Models	1200	1212	1224.12	1236.361	4872.4812
9	Garden	1800	1818	1836.18	1854.542	7308.7218
10	Total Monthly Sales	10600	10706	10813.06	10921.19	43040.2506
11						

Sheet1 / Sheet2 / Sheet3 / Sheet4 /

The formula that calculated the 1% growth in sales in the Trendy Toys plan produced results with varying numbers of decimal places. The formatting options in Excel can be used to change this. As a first example all the cells will be formatted to whole numbers, i.e. with zero decimal places.

6   Click on the sheet box to select the entire sheet.

7   Select *Format | Cells* which produces the dialogue box shown in Figure 4.2.

Figure 4.2.
Format Cells
dialogue box.

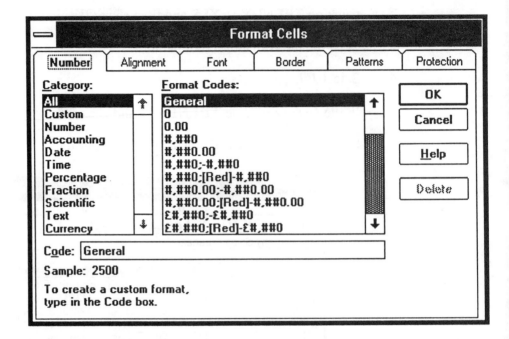

As you can see from this dialogue box cells can be formatted in six main areas, namely *Number, Alignment, Font, Border, Patterns,* and *protection.*

Within the *Number* tab there are 10 different categories, namely *Custom, Number, Accounting, Date, Time, Percentage, Fraction, Scientific, Text* and *Currency.* In addition to the 10 categories there is an *All* option. This displays all the formatting options in all the categories.

8   Change the *Category* to *Number.*

9   The first *Format Code* in this category is 0 which is what you want.

10   Click *OK* to apply the format to the worksheet. All subsequent entries into this worksheet will now be formatted to zero decimal places. Figure 4.3 is the plan with formatted cells.

Figure 4.3.
Plan with zero
decimal places.

	A	B	C	D	E	F
1	**TRENDY TOYS - London Branch**					
2	Quarterly Sales Forecast					
3						
4		January	February	March	April	Quarterly Total
5	Baby & Toddler	2500	2525	2550	2576	10151
6	Educational	2100	2121	2142	2164	8527
7	Dolls	3000	3030	3060	3091	12181
8	Models	1200	1212	1224	1236	4872
9	Garden	1800	1818	1836	1855	7309
10	Total Monthly Sales	10600	10706	10813	10921	43040
11						

TRENDY_2.XLS — Sheet1 / Sheet2 / Sheet3 / Sheet4

Numeric Formatting and Accuracy

Look closely at the figures for April and you will see that the values in the column do not add up to the value in the total cell - adding the column up manually produces a result of 10922 as opposed to 10921 which is displayed. This is because the formatting only affects the display, rounding each individual cell to the specified number of decimal places, but Excel continues to accurately evaluate formulae based on the full level of accuracy which is 16 significant decimal places.

You can change the level of accuracy, or *precision* as Excel refers to it.

1 Select *Tools | Options* and the *Calculation* tab.

2 Click on the *Precision as Displayed* box in the *Workbook Options* section of this dialogue box.

This will actually change the values in the cells to the number of decimal places currently being displayed and the truncated values will be used in subsequent calculations.

3 Click *OK*.

4 A message box is displayed warning you that *"Data will permanently lose accuracy"*.

5 Click *OK*.

The values in the worksheet are adjusted and if you manually add up the April figures they will match the total, although they differ from the values produced previously.

You can return to the original values by returning to the ***Tools | Options | Calculation*** dialogue box and clearing the *Precision as Displayed* box.

Tip: *You can access the Format Cells dialogue box quickly by selecting the cells to be formatted and then with the mouse pointer somewhere on the selection click the right mouse button. This produces a context sensitive Quick Menu, which contains an option to Format Cells.*

Exercise

> **1**   Return the formatting of the plan to General.
>
> **2**   Format all the numeric cells in the plan to two decimal places.
>
> **3**   Change the precision to reflect the two decimal places.
>
> **4**   Cancel the precision adjustment.

If you want three decimal places, click on *Number* in the *Category* list and then type **0.000** in the *Code* box. This will be displayed at the bottom of the *Format Codes* list and if you click on *Custom* in the *Category* list will also be listed there as a *Format Code*.

Currency Formatting

Two of the number formatting categories are concerned with currency, namely *Currency* and *Accounting*.

1   Select row 10 of the plan to format the totals with a currency symbol.

2   Select ***Format | Cells*** and click on *Currency*. Figure 4.4 shows the *Format Codes* options available.

*Figure 4.4.
Currency
formatting
options.*

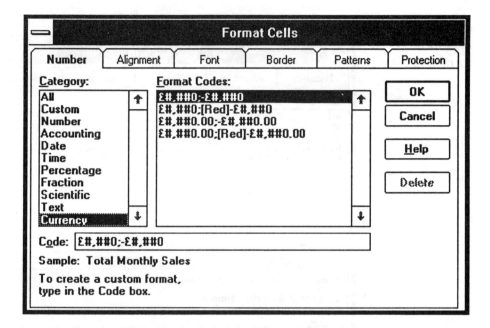

There are four options and each one shows you how positive and negative values are displayed. For example the first option has a currency symbol, a comma to separate thousands and zero decimal places, whereas the fourth option has a currency symbol, a command to separate thousands, two decimal places and negative values are displayed in red.

3 Click on the second option and click *OK*.

Note: *If you have dollar signs ($) and want pound signs (£) you can make a permanent change by opening the Windows Control Panel, in the Program Manager, and changing the Country specification in the International section. Alternatively you can enter your own Code in the Format Cells dialogue box to include an option for any currency symbol you require.*

Figure 4.5 shows the *Format Code* options for the *Accounting* category. The main difference between this and the *Currency* category is that spaces are included in the *Accounting* options so that the currency symbols line up in a column on the worksheet.

Figure 4.5.
Accounting
format codes.

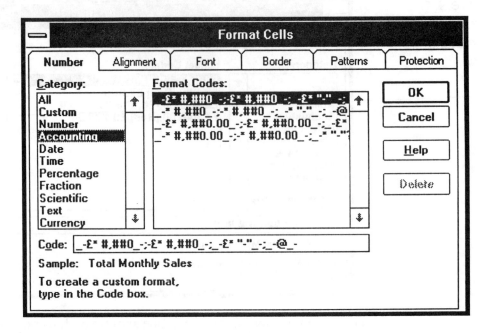

1   Select the range F5:F10.

2   Select *Format | Cells*.

3   Click on the *Accounting* category and accept the first *Format Code* option by clicking *OK*.

Tip: *If you want to adjust the column width of certain columns to improve the formatted display you can click on the column separator line where the column letters are displayed. When the pointer changes to a cross with arrow heads, click and drag right or left to increase or decrease the column width.*

Figure 4.6 shows the effect of this formatting option and the difference between *Currency* and *Accounting*.

*Figure 4.6.
Plan with
currency and
accounting
codes.*

	A	B	C	D	E	F
	TRENDY TOYS - London Branch					
1						
2	Quarterly Sales Forecast					
3						
4		January	February	March	April	Quarterly Total
5	Baby & Toddler	2500.00	2525.00	2550.25	2575.75	£ 10,151
6	Educational	2100.00	2121.00	2142.21	2163.63	£ 8,527
7	Dolls	3000.00	3030.00	3060.30	3090.90	£ 12,181
8	Models	1200.00	1212.00	1224.12	1236.36	£ 4,872
9	Garden	1800.00	1818.00	1836.18	1854.54	£ 7,309
10	Total Monthly Sales	£10,600	£10,706	£10,813	£10,921	£ 43,040
11						

Title bar: TRENDY_2.XLS

Sheet tabs: **Sheet1** / Sheet2 / Sheet3 / Sheet4

Formatting Buttons

The Formatting toolbar has a number of predefined buttons that allow you to quickly assign common formats to selected cells. The following describes what each button will do to a selected range of cells.

Currency Style button which formats to *accounting* with two decimal places

Percent Style button which formats to percent with no decimals.

Comma Style button which formats with commas separating thousands with two decimal places.

Increase Decimal button which increases the number of decimal places by one each time you click the button.

Decrease Decimal button which decreases the number of decimal places by one each time you click the button.

Exercise

1   Select all the numeric cells and format them to simple integer values.

Exercise cont.

2	Using the buttons format the **Total Monthly Sales** to *Accounting* with one decimal place. (You may have to increase the column widths in order to see the formatted cells as the default width is too small).
3	Format the **Quarterly Totals** to *Comma* with zero decimal places.
4	Return the formatting for all cells to simple whole numbers.

Format Painter

Having formatted a range of cells the *Format Painter* button [🖌] on the Standard toolbar allows existing formatting to be applied to another cell or range of cells.

1   Select the range B10:F10.

2   Click on the *Currency Style* button [💲] and reduce the number of decimal places to zero using the *Decrease Decimal* [.00] button.

3   With the range still highlighted click on the *Format Painter* button [🖌]. When the mouse pointer is moved there is a paintbrush to the left of it.

4   Now select the range F5:F9 and when the mouse button is released the currency formatting is automatically copied to this range.

If another range is also to be formatted in this way, click again on the *Format Painter* button and select the range to be formatted.

Exercise

1	Select all the numeric cells and format them to simple integer values.
2	Format the range B10:F10 to currency with zero decimals.
3	Use the *Format Painter* to repeat this format on the range F5.F9.

Exercise cont.

4	Save the file with the name TRENDY_F.

Formatting the Plan as a Whole

The formatting options discussed so far in this chapter have been concerned with the way values are displayed. Excel also offers a wide range of formatting options for other aspects of the worksheet. These include the way text is displayed in terms of font, point size etc., adding borders and shading to cells and protecting cells.

In Chapter Three you applied some text formatting using the font box, point size and the *Bold* and *Italic* buttons on the Formatting toolbar. The other buttons on the this toolbar allow you to adjust the alignment of cell contents, to add borders to cells and to change the colour of various worksheet areas. A brief description of these buttons follows:

Align Left button which is the default setting for text entries, but can be applied to cells containing values.

Centre button which centres text or values in the cell.

Align Right button which is the default setting for values, but can be applied to any cell.

Centre Across Columns button centres text or values across a selected range of columns.

For example, to centre the two titles in cells A1 and A2 of Trendy Toys:

1 Ensure you are working with TRENDY_F which is the partially formatted version of the plan created in the previous exercise.

2 Select the range A1:F2

3 Click on the *Centre Across Columns* button. Figure 4.7 shows the effect of this formatting on the plan.

Figure 4.7.
Titles centred
across the plan.

	A	B	C	D	E	F	
			TRENDY_F.XLS				
1		**TRENDY TOYS - London Branch**					
2			Quarterly Sales Forecast				
3							
4		January	February	March		April	Quarterly Total
5	Baby & Toddler	2500	2525	2550	2576	£	10,151
6	Educational	2100	2121	2142	2164	£	8,527
7	Dolls	3000	3030	3060	3091	£	12,181
8	Models	1200	1212	1224	1236	£	4,872
9	Garden	1800	1818	1836	1855	£	7,309
10	Total Monthly Sales	£ 10,600	£ 10,706	£ 10,813	£ 10,921	£	43,040
11							

Sheet1 / Sheet2 / Sheet3 / Sheet4 / She

Borders can be selectively placed around cells using the *Borders* button.

1   Select the range A4:F10.

2   Click on the arrow to the right of the *Borders* button. Figure 4.8 shows the options that are displayed.

Figure 4.8.
Borders options

3   Click on the bottom right button to put a bold border around the selected range.

4   Click outside the plan to deselect the range.

5   Select the range B10:F10.

6   Click on the arrow by the *Borders* button.

7   Click on the middle right button.

8   Select the range A4:A10.

9   Click on the arrow by the *Borders* button.

10   Click on the top right button [⬚].

The month headings would stand out better if the cells were shaded.

1   Select the range B4:F4.

2   Click on the arrow to the right of the *Color* button [▦▾] .

3   Select the fourth option ▦.

4   If you are working on a monochrome monitor you will have a light shading applied to the cells. With a colour monitor the cells are shaded light green.
As a result of shading the cells the text has been reversed and therefore the colour should be adjusted.

1   Click on the arrow to the right of the *Font Color* button [▦▾] and select the first option ▦.
Figure 4.9 shows how the above formatting has affected the plan.

Figure 4.9.
Formatted Plan.

	A	B	C	D	E	F
	TRENDY TOYS - London Branch					
2	Quarterly Sales Forecast					
3						
4						
5	Baby & Toddler	2500	2525	2550	2576	£ 10,151
6	Educational	2100	2121	2142	2164	£ 8,527
7	Dolls	3000	3030	3060	3091	£ 12,181
8	Models	1200	1212	1224	1236	£ 4,872
9	Garden	1800	1818	1836	1855	£ 7,309
10	Total Monthly Sales	£ 10,600	£ 10,706	£ 10,813	£ 10,921	£ 43,040
11						

Sheet1 / Sheet2 / Sheet3 / Sheet4 / She

Note: *Be careful with your use of colour if you intend to print the plan and do not have a colour printer. Excessive shading can be very slow to print and is not always as attractive on paper as it appears to be on screen.*

Exercise

1   Re-open TRENDY_F.XLS.

2   Using the buttons on the Formatting toolbar, format the plan to
appear as shown in Figure 4.10 below.

Figure 4.10.
Fully formatted
plan.

TRENDY TOYS - London Branch					
Quarterly Sales Forecast					
	January	February	March	April	Quarterly Total
Baby & Toddler	2500	2525	2550	2576	£ 10,151
Educational	2100	2121	2142	2164	£ 8,527
Dolls	3000	3030	3060	3091	£ 12,181
Models	1200	1212	1224	1236	£ 4,872
Garden	1800	1818	1836	1855	£ 7,309
Total Monthly Sales	£ 10,600	£ 10,706	£ 10,813	£ 10,921	£ 43,040

Note: *Although the buttons on the Formatting toolbar provide most of the
options you will regularly require, further options for adjusting alignment,
adding borders and shading are available through the Format Cells
dialogue box which has tabs for Alignment, Font, Border, Patters and
Protection.*

AutoFormat

Formatting in the way shown above is effective, but can be time consuming
as there are so many options to choose from. You can quickly format a plan
or section of a plan using the built-in AutoFormat feature.

1   Re-open TRENDY_F.XLS.

2   Select the entire plan by clicking on cell A1 and then click and drag to cell
F10.

3   Select *Format | AutoFormat* which displays the dialogue box in Figure
4.11.

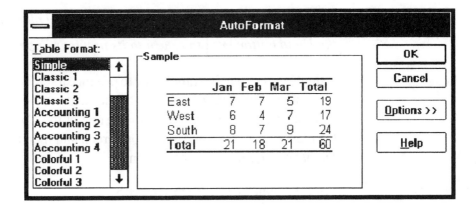

Figure 4.11.
AutoFormat
dialogue box.

4 Click on some of the options in the *Table Format* list which will give you an example of the formatting in the *Sample* section of the dialogue box.

5 Select *Classic 1* and click *OK*.

Figure 4.12 shows the effect of applying this format option.

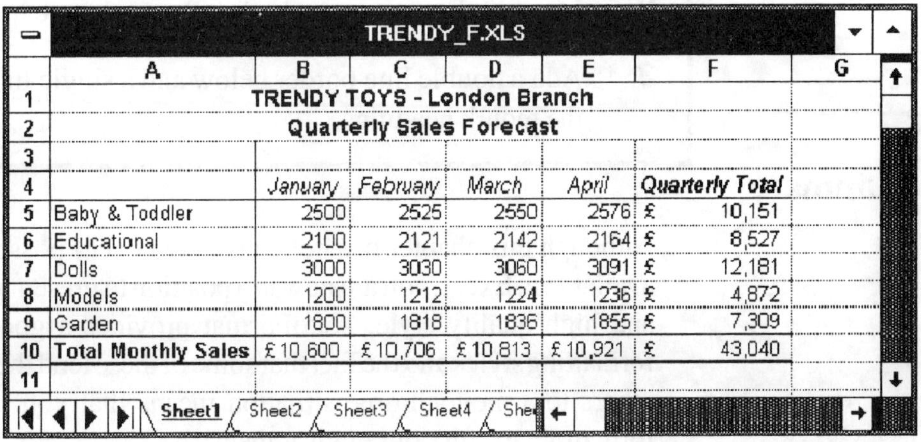

Figure 4.12.
Classic 1
AutoFormat.

Any numeric formatting that was in place remains as you set it, but the text formatting that was applied when the plan was created in Chapter Three has been replaced with the preset formats of the *Classic 1* style.

You can add or delete areas of formatting using the buttons on the Formatting toolbar if you are not entirely happy with the preset formats.

Tip: *If you decide you do not like the formatted plan at all you can click on the Undo button* ↰ *to return to its previous appearance.*

Using AutoFormat is a quick way to produce a screen version and a printable version of your plan. If you are working with a colour screen, but only have a black and white printer you can use one of the *Colorful* options to format the plan whilst you work with it on screen and then format it with either the *Simple* or *Classic* style for printing.

6   Save the plan as TRENDY_M.XLS.

Note: *TRENDY_M.XLS will become the master plan that will be used as the basis of examples later in the book.*

Exercise

> **1**   Reopen TRENDY_F.XLS.
>
> **2**   Use AutoFormat to apply the Classic 3 style to the plan.
>
> **3**   Add a double line border below and a single line border above the month headings.

Summary

Although this chapter has not considered every possible formatting option available in Excel, you are now in a position to present plans in a professional and high quality style. AutoFormat provides a good selection of preset formatting styles and the fact that some of these lend themselves to colour and others to a monochrome situation means that you can easily change the formatting to suit your environment.

Self Test

1   To what accuracy are numbers displayed by default?

2   To what accuracy are numbers calculated by default?

3   What are the disadvantages of using the General format?

4 What are the differences between Accounting and Currency formats?

5 What effect does the *Precision As Displayed* option on the *Calculation* tab of the Options dialogue box have on the worksheet calculations?

6 How do you define a format that shows positive numbers with commas separating the thousands and four decimal places?

7 How can you amend this format to show negative numbers in parentheses?

8 In addition to using the *Borders* button, how can you apply a border to a range of cells?

9 What is the easiest way to apply a border around every cell in a range, rather than an outline around the entire range?

10 How can you format a cell to show reversed-out text, i.e. white letters on a black background?

FIVE
Printing Plans

Key Learning Points In This Chapter

- Print a plan using the Print menu and the Print button

- Print selected sections of a plan

- Use Print Preview to view the plan

- Set headers and footers

- Set print titles

- Print formulae

Introduction

Two files will be used in this chapter in order to practice the Print features of Word. Initially the TRENDY_M document that you created in Chapter Three will be opened and printed. A longer plan called YEARDATA.XLS will be created to illustrate the *Print* | *Preview* command and the page layout options available.

Printing a Plan

Plans in Excel must first be opened before they can be printed.

1 Using the *Open* button, ensure that the STEPXL directory is current and open the file TRENDY_M.

Printing can be initiated either by clicking on the *Print* button 🖨 or by selecting *File* | *Print*.

2 To print all of TRENDY_M on the default printer, click on the *Print* button and the file will be printed directly.

There are no messages or prompts when the *Print* button is used and the whole file will always be printed.

3 Print TRENDY_M again, but using the Print dialogue box.

4 Select *File* | *Print* which will produce the dialogue box shown in Figure 5.1.

The printer that is listed in this box is the default printer that is established when setting up Windows. This printer choice may be changed by clicking on *Printer Setup* in the Print dialogue box which will display the available printers as may be seen in Figure 5.2. It is important to ensure that your computer is connected, either directly or through the network, to the printer you choose to use. In most cases, if your system has been set up correctly the default printer will be the correct choice.

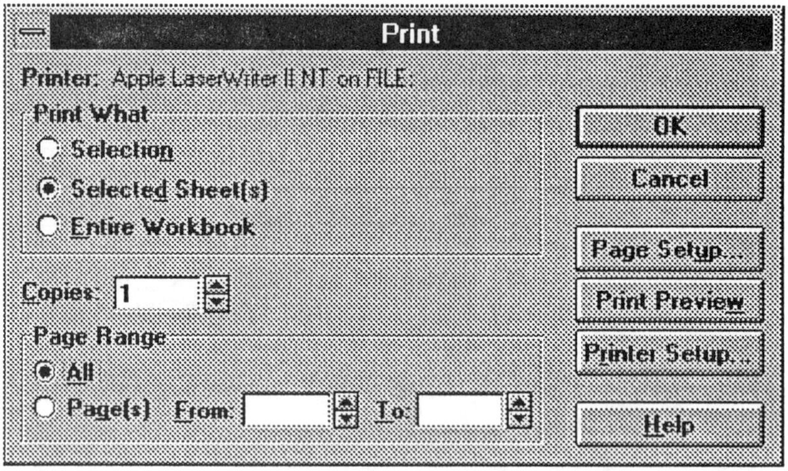

Figure 5.1.
Print dialogue
box.

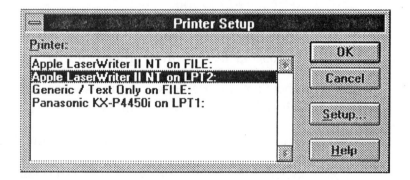

Figure 5.2.
Printer Setup
dialogue box.

The other sections of the print dialogue box allow you to specify exactly what you want to print, how many copies you wish to print and which pages of a long plan you want. The default selection is to print one copy of the current worksheet, but you can choose to print a selected range of a sheet or the entire workbook.

5   In the first instance the default settings are all correct so it is only necessary to either press ENTER or click *OK* to commence printing the plan.

Creating a Plan to Print

In order to see the benefits of some of the other printing options, a simple daily stock records plan for January to April will be created.

Open a new workbook by clicking on the *New* button [□].

1   Type the following:

A1   **Total Stock Held Per Day for Trendy Toys, London**

A2   **January-April**

A3   **Item Number**

2   Select the range A1:H3 and click the *Center Across Columns* button. This will centre the headings on the screen.

3   A reference to 1 January will be entered into cell A5.

A5   **1/1**

When you make the entry into cell A5 Excel will interpret 1/1 as *01-Jan* and this will be displayed in the cell.

AutoFill can now be used to complete the remaining dates.

4   Click on the *Fill Handle* and drag to cell A124 which will be the 30 April.

5   Item numbers of 1 through 10 need to be entered in row 4.

B4   **1**

C4   **2**

6   Select cells B4 and C4 and then drag on the *Fill Handle* to extend the range to K4.

Simulated data will be entered into the worksheet to represent the amount of stock held. This can quickly be created using the RAND function. A formula will be entered that generates integer random numbers between 1 and 150.

7   B5=INT(1+RAND()*(150-1))

8   Click on the *Fill Handle* and drag to cell B124.

9   Release the mouse button and with the range still highlighted, click again on the *Fill Handle* and drag to cell K124.

The range is filled with random numbers between 1 and 150, but the numbers will change each time the worksheet is recalculated and the RAND() function is re-evaluated. Therefore as the formula is no longer required it will be replaced with absolute values.

10   Select the range A1:K124

Tip: *A keyboard shortcut way of selecting this range is, with B5 as the active cell, hold down SHIFT+END, SHIFT+HOME*

11   Select *Edit | Copy*

12   Select *Edit | Paste Special*

13   Click on *Values* and click *OK*.

14   Press ENTER to complete the copy.

Figure 5.3 shows the top left screen of this file. (Remember that the numbers in your plan will be different due to the use of the RAND() function.

15   Save the plan by clicking on the *Save* button 🖫.

16   Ensure you are in the STEPXL directory and in the *Name* box, type **YEARDATA**

17   Click *OK* to complete the save.

Figure 5.3.
Beginning of a
three page
document.

	A	B	C	D	E	F	G	H
1		Total Stock Held Per Day for Trendy Toys, London						
2		January-April						
3		Item Number						
4		1	2	3	4	5	6	7
5	01-Jan	85	45	28	5	23	30	14
6	02-Jan	46	61	12	92	126	147	149
7	03-Jan	116	5	83	15	114	25	128
8	04-Jan	41	111	50	100	149	13	141
9	05-Jan	20	46	8	84	86	42	13
10	06-Jan	81	66	55	99	42	72	37
11	07-Jan	136	50	103	138	101	17	90
12	08-Jan	21	143	26	131	130	122	129
13	09-Jan	39	72	61	47	66	85	3
14	10-Jan	55	91	117	1	63	58	53

Printing a Large Plan

Before looking at the options for coping with large plans, click on the *Print* button and see how this larger plan is printed. If you are printing on A4 paper it will be six pages long with 55 lines on each page. Columns A through H will be printed on pages 1 to 3 and columns I through K will be on pages 4 to 6.

Note: *If you want to change the print order so that lines 1-55 for columns A through H will be following by lines 1-55 for columns I through K, select File | Page Setup and select the Sheet tab. Click on the Across, then Down in the Page Order section of the dialogue box.*

Printing Selected Parts of the Plan

1   Select the range A4:K35 which represents the January data.

2   Access the Print dialogue box by selecting *File | Print*.

You can now specify which sections of the document you wish to print together with the number of copies required. For example, to print two copies of the January data:-

3   Click on *Selection* in the *Print What* section of the dialogue box.

4   Click on the up arrow to the right of the *Copies* box to display 2.

5   Click on *OK* to print the pages.

Unless you change the settings, Excel will print 55 standard height lines and eight standard width columns on an A4 page of paper.

To print one copy of pages 1 and 2 of this plan:

1   Select *File | Print*.

2   Click on *Pages*.

3   Type **1** in the *From* box and **2** in the *To* box.

4   Click on *OK* to print the pages.

The effect of printing pages one and two is to print the range A1:I55 on the first page and J1:K55 on the second page.

Setting a Print Area

In the above examples the area to print has been highlighted on the screen and the *Selection* option in the Print dialogue box taken. The problem with this approach is that once you deselect the area the print range is lost. You can set a more permanent print area if you are regularly going to print the same part of a worksheet through the *Print Area* option on the *Sheet* tab of the Page Setup dialogue box.

1   Select *File | Page Setup* and select the *Sheet* tab.

2   Click in the *Print Area* edit box

3   Either type in the range to be printed or select the range with the mouse (you can do this while the dialogue box is on the screen).

Tip: *If you want to move the dialogue box out of the way while you select the print area, click on the title bar and drag the box somewhere else on the screen.*

A worksheet can only have one Print Area at a time, but you do not have to delete one before creating another.

Page Breaks

As soon as you have printed all or part of a plan, Excel inserts automatic page breaks which are shown on the screen by a dotted line. (If you scroll down to line 56 you will see the first page break after line 55). If you do not want to see these you can disable the display by selecting *Tools | Options* and the *View* tab. Clear the *Automatic Page Breaks* box.

You can insert page breaks at any point in the worksheet through the *Insert | Page Break* command. A dotted line is inserted across the entire row above the active cell. If you select *Insert* with the active cell in the row below the page break the page break option has changed to *Remove Page Break* and you can select this to remove a page break you no longer require.

To insert a page break after the January data:

1   Click on cell A36 (any cell on row 36 would do)

2   Select *Insert | Page Break*

The above procedure inserts both a horizontal and vertical page break. Sometimes you might want to manually insert only a vertical or only a horizontal break.

To insert a vertical page break after five columns:

1   Click on the *Column Heading* for column F to select the column.

2   Select *Insert | Page Break*

A vertical dotted line is displayed to indicate that the page will be broken at this point.

Once you have inserted page breaks, the automatic page breaks are adjusted. There will be a break 55 lines after the manually inserted page break, unless you insert another manual break.

Scale to Fit

If you want to print the range A4:K35 on one page you can ask Excel to reduce the font size to fit a selected range on a specified number of pages. In this case you must first select the range to be reduced.

1   Select the range A1:K55.

2   Select *File | Print.*

3   Click the *Selection* button.

4   Click on the *Page Setup* box and on the *Page* tab which produces the dialogue box shown in Figure 5.4.

Figure 5.4
Page Setup
dialogue box

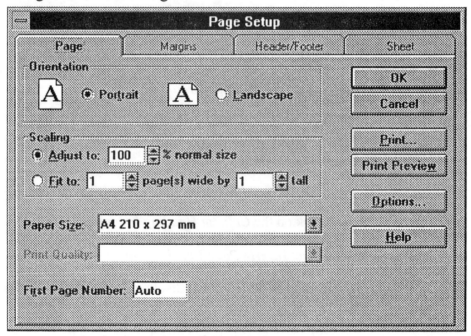

In the *Scaling* section you can either specify the percentage of normal size that you want to make the printout, or you can click the *Fit to* button and specify the number of pages in terms of width and height that you want the range to be printed on.

5   Click the *Fit To* button.

6 Click *OK*. To return to the Print dialogue box and click *OK* to commence printing.

Exercise

---

1 Reopen YEARDATA.XLS

2 Print two copies of the data for February

3 Print one copy of the same range on a single page.

Print Preview

In order to see how the plan will look before it is printed you can use the *Print Preview* window. This allows the overall appearance of one or more pages to be seen. Although it is hard to read in some cases, particularly if you have scaled the plan to fit on fewer pages, you can see where data falls on the page in relation to margins and page breaks.

Tip: *Taking the time to preview a plan can ultimately save time by reducing the number of times you need to print a file before getting the layout absolutely correct.*

Print Preview may be accessed either by clicking on the *Print Preview* button , by selecting *File | Print Preview* or by clicking on the *Print Preview* box from within the Print dialogue box.

1 Select *File | Print*

2 Click on the *Page Setup* box

3 Reset the scaling factor to 100% and click OK.

4 Click on the *Print Preview* box.

Figure 5.5 shows the Print Preview screen.

Figure 5.5.
Print Preview.

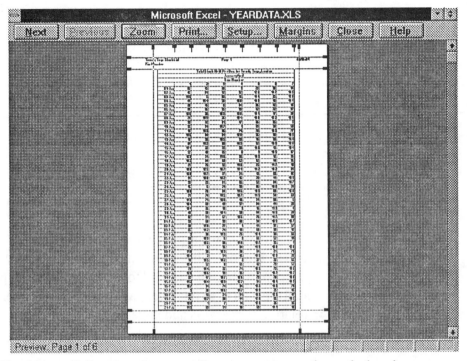

The *Next* and *Previous* buttons allow you to page through the plan.

The *Zoom* button toggles between a full page and magnified display. If you move the mouse pointer into the display area it will change to a magnifying glass.

The *Print* button will print the plan with the current settings.

The *Setup* button accesses the Page Setup dialogue box seen above.

The *Margins* button allows you to change the margin settings.

1   Position the magnifying glass pointer towards the bottom of the first page and click once.

The effect of this is to zoom in on that section of the plan.

2   Click the *Margins* button. A series of markers are displayed around the document. These represent top, bottom, left and right margins as well as header and footer markers and column dividers.

3   Position the mouse pointer on the top left marker and it will change to a cross.

4   Click and drag up or down to increase or decrease the margin. The actual margin size is displayed at the bottom left of the screen.

5   Click again on the *Margins* button to remove the markers.

6   Click on *Close* to exit Print Preview and return to the worksheet.

If you go to the Page Setup dialogue box you can click on the *Margins* tab to see the actual settings for the margins and you can manually change them here.

There is a check box on the Margins dialogue box for centring a printout on the page. It is usually preferable to check this so that your plan is centred at least horizontally, if not vertically on the page. On a multiple page document, if the last page is not complete, vertical centring will place that part of the plan centrally on the page.

Exercise

1   Re-open YEARDATA.XLS.

2   Using Print Preview put a two inch margin all around the plan.

3   Print two copies of page one.

Headers and Footers

Headers and footers are reserved areas at the top and bottom of a page into which you can enter text and insert page numbers, date and time. Any information that you put into a header or footer is automatically printed on each page of a printout.

1   Select *File | Print*

2   Click on the *Page Setup* box and then the *Header/Footer* tab. Figure 5.6 shows the Header/Footer dialogue box.

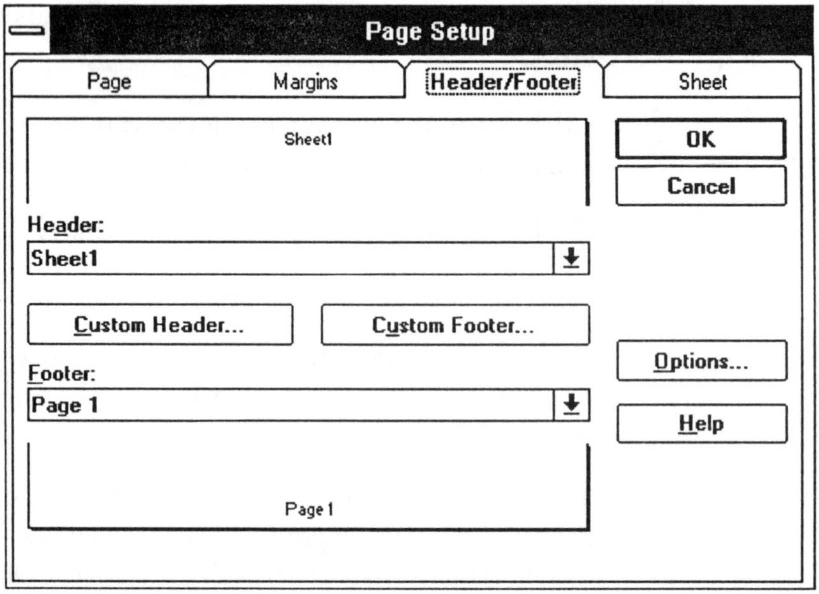

Figure 5.6.
Header/Footer
dialogue box.

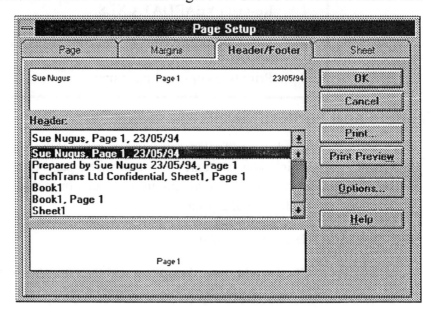

The default settings are a Sheet reference centred as the header and the page number centred as a footer. There are a number of built-in options for headers and footers and you can view these by clicking on the arrows to the right of the *Header* and *Footer* boxes. Figure 5.7 shows the current header list.

Figure 5.7.
Built-in header
options.

Clicking on one of the options displays a sample in the dialogue box. In Figure 5.7 the name and company listed is the user name and company name used when Excel was installed. You can change the user name by selecting **Tools | Options** and the *General* tab. At the bottom of the dialogue box the *User Name* is displayed and can be changed.

If the built-in options are not suitable you can create your own headers and footers by selecting *Custom Header* or *Custom Footer* from the Header/ Footer dialogue box. Figure 5.8 shows the Header dialogue box.

Figure 5.8
Header dialogue
box.

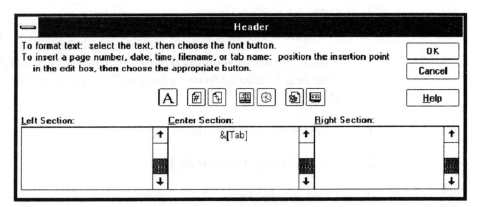

As you can see in Figure 5.8, three sections can be specified on a header or footer. The *Left Section* is left-justified, the *Center Section* is centred on the page and the *Right Section* is right-justified. You can type text into any section, pressing ALT+ENTER for a new line. The buttons in the centre of the dialogue box are used to format the text, and to insert special values into the header or footer.

The buttons perform the following functions:

 Format font. Select the text, click the button and then specify formatting options.

 Page number. Inserts &[Page] but when printed will display the page number.

Number of pages. Inserts the total number of pages in the selected print range.

Current date. Inserts the current system date.

Current time. Inserts the current system time.

Workbook name. Inserts the filename the workbook is saved under.

Worksheet name. Inserts the worksheet reference that is displayed on the sheet tabs.

Tip: *If you are developing a plan and producing lots of printouts include the time in a header or footer which will ensure you know the latest version of the plan.*

1   Click in the *Left Section*

2   Type **Trendy Toys Stock List**

3   Press ALT+ENTER

4   Type **First Quarter**

5   Click in the *Center Section*

6   Double click to select the current text and press DEL to delete it.

7   Type **Page** and press the SPACEBAR once.

8   Click the page number button.

9   Click in the *Right Section*.

10 Click the date button.

11 Click *OK* to return to the Page Setup dialogue box

12 Click on the arrow to the right of the Footer box and scroll to the top of the list in order to select [none].

13 Click the *Print Preview* button to see the effect of the header.

Tip: *If you want to set headers and footers without printing you can select File | Page Setup directly instead of going through the Print command.*

Exercise

1 Reopen YEARDATA.XLS.

2 Put the following information as a footer:

Page # of ##   Trendy Toys   Date

3 Clear any existing header data.

Print Titles

When printing a multiple page plan it is sometimes useful to repeat certain information on every page. For example, with the YEARDATA plan it would be useful to have the dates repeated when the later columns are printed and the item numbers repeated when later rows are printed. This is achieved by setting *Print Titles*:

1 Select *File | Page Setup* and select the *Sheet* tab.

2 Click in the *Rows to Repeat at Top* edit box.

3 Select rows 1:4 by clicking in the *Row Header* for row 1 and dragging to row 4 on the worksheet (you can do this while the dialogue box is on the screen).

4 Click in the *Columns to Repeat at Left* edit box.

5 Select column A by clicking in the *Column Header*.

6 Click *OK*.

Having set Print Titles it is important not to include column A and row 4 in the print area. Therefore to print the January data you should select the range B5:K35.

Exercise

1 Reopen YEARDATA.XLS

2 Print the March data with date and item numbers repeated on all pages of the printout.

Printing Formulae

A useful piece of documentation for a plan is to retain a printout of the formulae instead of the results.

1   Select *Tools | Options* and select the *View* tab.

2   Click the *Formulas* checkbox.

3   Print the plan.

Note: *It is particularly useful to set Print Titles before printing the formulae as it is likely to spread over several pages.*

Summary

In this chapter you have learnt how to print plans in their entirety and to select ranges and pages. The ability to scale the size of a printout gives you considerable control over the final output. Using Print Preview to look at the appearance of your document and adjust the margins on the screen before you print it avoids having trailing rows and columns.

Self Test

1   Suggest two ways of printing the entire plan.

2   What is required to print pages 2 and 6 of a plan?

3   How can you print a selected range of a plan?

4   What is the quickest way to access Print Preview?

5   How can you see the margin size as you adjust it?

6   How do you clear the automatic page breaks?

7   How can you reduce the size of a plan to fit on fewer pages ?

8   What is required to create a customised header?

9   What must you take into account when printing a range having set print titles?

10   How do you print the formulae behind the values in a range?

SIX
Multiple Sheets and Files

Key Learning Points In This Chapter

- Manipulating several worksheets in a workbook

- Consolidating data using a workbook

- Linking data between workbooks

- Saving the workspace

Introduction

So far in this book all the exercises have been based on a single worksheet. However, one of the more powerful features of Excel is the ability to work with several worksheets at one time - in the form of a workbook. In fact, in Excel 5.0 all files are referred to as workbooks even if you are only using a single worksheet. By default you have 16 worksheets available to you in any workbook, named Sheet 1 through Sheet 16. The maximum number of worksheets you can have in a workbook is 255. The sheet names are displayed on tabs at the bottom of the screen. The name of the active sheet is always in bold. You can also have different types of sheets in a workbook in the form of *worksheets, chart sheets* and *macro sheets.*

In addition to workbooks, Excel allows you to link data between different Excel files - and indeed files in other applications. In this chapter you will learn how to work with multiple sheet workbooks and how to link data between different Excel files. Linking data with other applications is discussed in Chapter Twelve.

Workbooks

You have considerable control over the way you use a workbook. You can insert new sheets, delete or rename sheets, move or copy sheets within a workbook or to other workbooks and you can hide sheets. In fact you can do most of the things you do with a cell or range of cells with a sheet or series of sheets in a workbook.

Excel recognises six different types of sheet in a workbook:

Worksheet	Used to enter text and data and perform calculations.
Chart sheet	Used to create charts that are not embedded in a worksheet.
Visual Basic Module	Used to develop systems with the Excel Visual Basic programming language.

Dialog	Used to develop systems with the Excel Visual Basic programming language.
Excel 4.0 macro sheet	Provides compatibility with macros developed in the earlier version of Excel.
Excel 4.0 International macro sheet	Provides compatibility with macros developed in the earlier version of Excel.

Creating a Multi-Sheet Workbook

The original plan developed for Trendy Toys in Chapter Three was a sales forecast for the London Branch. Trendy Toys also has branches in Manchester, Dundee and Belfast and in this chapter a workbook will be created with sales forecasts for all branches together with a consolidation sheet showing the total forecast sales for each product category.

1   Close any workbooks that might currently be open.

2   Open TRENDY_M.XLS.

3   Select *File | Save As* and type the name **TRENDY_N** to indicate that this is the National sales forecast for Trendy Toys.

4   Position the mouse pointer on the *Sheet 1* tab and click the right mouse button. This accesses the shortcut menu.

5   From the menu select *Rename.* (You could have selected *Format | Sheet | Rename* to access the same dialogue box).

6   Type **London** into the edit box of the Rename Sheet dialogue box and click *OK*.

7   Click on the tab for *Sheet 2* and repeat the above procedure to name this sheet Manchester. Name sheets 3 and 4 Dundee and Belfast respectively.

8   Click on the *London* tab to return to the plan.

Moving Between Sheets

You can quickly activate any worksheet by clicking on the sheet tab. For example to go to the *Dundee* sheet, click on the *Dundee Name* tab. However, as you cannot see all the available sheets, there are a series of tab scrolling buttons which control the sheet tabs that are displayed.

Moves to the first tab in the workbook.

Moves to the previous tab (left).

Moves to the next tab (right).

Moves to the last tab in the workbook.

Copying To Other Sheets

The London worksheet can be copied into the other sheets and the data removed in preparation for entering new data for the other branches.

1 Select the range A1:F10.

2 Click the Copy button.

3 Activate the second sheet by clicking on *Manchester*.

4 Hold down the SHIFT key and click on the *Belfast* tab.

The word [Group] appears next to the file name on the title bar at the top of the screen.

5 Press ENTER or click on the *Paste* button

The Manchester, Dundee and Belfast sheets are now grouped and the copy is performed on each sheet. Once sheets are grouped you can perform a number of common tasks, including:

- Enter column titles and formulas that will automatically be entered into all the grouped sheets.

- Format cells and ranges on the grouped sheets.

- Hide or delete the grouped sheets.

Although the cell formatting has been copied from the original sheet, the column widths have not been adjusted. With grouping on and with Manchester as the active sheet (click on the *Manchester* tab to make it active), widen columns A and F.

1   Click on the separator bar on the *Column header* and drag to increase the column width until the full title is displayed.

2   Repeat this procedure with column F.

If you click on any of the grouped sheets you will see that the column widths have been applied to them all.

Note: *At this stage London is not grouped.*

Different data is required for Manchester, Dundee and Belfast and so the existing data that was copied from London must be deleted. With grouping still on the data in all the sheets can be deleted in one operation.

3   Select the range B5:E9 and press DEL. The totals do not need to be deleted as the same formula will be required when the new data and formulae are entered.

4   Ungroup the sheets by positioning the mouse pointer on one of the grouped tabs and press the right mouse button to display the shortcut menu. Select *Ungroup Sheets*.

5   Edit cell A1 of the Manchester, Dundee and Belfast sheets to change the London reference in the title to the appropriate town.

6   Save the changes so far by clicking on the *Save* button ▇.

7   Enter the data and formulae listed below into the three new sheets:

The growth rate is used as part of the formula in column C. Therefore in cell B5 of the Manchester sheet you would enter **=B5*1.0075**. You can then use *AutoFill* to copy the formula down the range C5:C9 and across to cell F9.

Manchester	B&T	Educ	Dolls	Mod	Gard
January Data	1500	1750	1600	1800	2000
Growth rate	0.75%				
Dundee					
January Data	1350	1250	1400	1450	1600
Growth rate	1.02%				
Belfast					
January Data	1680	1730	1500	1200	1750
Growth rate	0.80%				

Displaying Multiple Worksheets

To see all or some of the sheets on the screen at the same time you can create new windows in which different sheets can be displayed.

1 With London as the active sheet select *Window | New.*

2 Repeat this two more times so that you have four windows in total.

   If you click on the *Window* menu you will see the four windows listed with the names TRENDY_N.XLS:1, TRENDY_N.XLS:2 etc. At this stage each window is displaying the London sheet.

3 Select *Window | Arrange | Tile* in order to display all four windows on the screen.

   Only one window is active at a time and this is indicated by the title bar which is highlighted. To change the active window click the mouse somewhere in the window you want to make active.

4 Click in the window named TRENDY_N.XLS:2 and then click the *Manchester* tab to display this sheet in the window.

5   Click in the window named TRENDY_N.XLS:3 and click the *Dundee* tab.

6   Click in the window named TRENDY_N.XLS:4 and click the *Belfast* tab.

Figure 6.1 shows how the screen will appear.

Figure 6.1.
Tiled Windows
showing four
worksheets

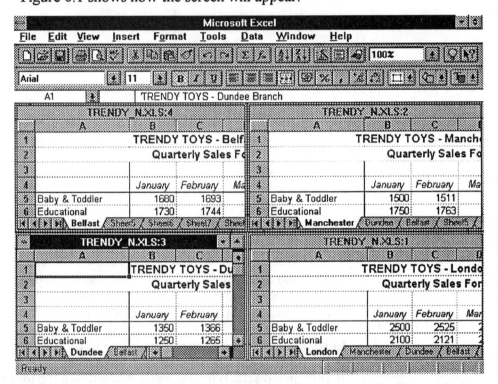

These four windows have all the attributes that you are familiar with on a single worksheet window. You can view different tabs and you can maximise or minimise any window. If you maximise a window you will no longer be able to see the other windows and you will have to select these through the *Window* command. If you minimise a window it is displayed at the bottom of the screen as a workbook icon. You can restore a minimised workbook by double-clicking on the icon.

To close a window you double click on the workbook *Control-menu* box illustrated in Chapter One. This action will only close a workbook if it is not being displayed in other windows.

1   Double click on the *Control-menu* box of the active window (it doesn't matter which one this is).

2   Close two other windows in the same way.

3   Maximise the window you are left with by clicking on the *Maximise* button at the top right of the screen and click on the *London* tab to make it active.

Creating a Summary Report

A new sheet will be inserted at the beginning of the TRENDY_N workbook which will consist of the total forecast sales for all the branches of Trendy Toys.

1   With the active cell somewhere on the London sheet select ***Insert | Worksheet.***

2   A new *Sheet 1* is inserted.

3   With the mouse pointer on the sheet tab click the right mouse button and select **Rename**. Type the name **Totals** and click *OK*.

Copying Titles and Formats

The titles can be copied from one of the branch sheets.

1   Click on the *London* tab.

2   Select the range A1:F4.

3   · Click the *Copy* button.

4   Click the *Totals* sheet tab.

5   Click on cell A1 and press ENTER to paste the cells.

6   Repeat the procedure for the range A3:A10.

7   Widen columns A and F to display the titles.

Some of the line formatting has been copied and some has not. An option when copying cells is to only paste the cell formats as opposed to their contents.

8   Click on the *London* sheet tab and Select the range A3:F10.

9   Click on the *Copy* button.

10   Click on the *Totals* sheet tab and click in cell A3.

11   Select **Edit | Paste | Special** and click the *Formats* option in the *Paste* section of the dialogue box.

12   Click *OK*.

Figure 6.2 shows the options in the Paste Special dialogue box.

Figure 6.2.
Paste Special
dialogue box.

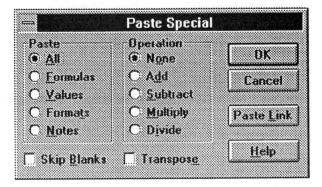

The default selection is to paste all the attributes that a cell has. This can be a formatted value, text, a formula or notes assigned to a cell. In addition you can perform arithmetic operations at the time of copying.

Edit the title to read **Trendy Toys** on the first line and **National Quarterly Sales Forecast** on the second line.

Creating the totals

A formula is required in cell B5 of the *Totals* sheet that sums cell B5 in the other sheets.

1   Click in cell B5 on the *Totals* sheet and click the *AutoSum* button Σ.

2   This will display =SUM() in cell B5.

3   Click on the *London* tab and click in cell B5.

4   Hold down the SHIFT key and click on the *Belfast* tab.

5   The formula bar now reads **=SUM(London:Belfast!B5)**

6   Press ENTER to complete the formula and the display will return to the *Totals* sheet.

This formula may be interpreted as sum cell B5 in sheets *London* through *Belfast*. Notice that the sheet range is separated by a colon, just like an ordinary cell range, and the cell reference is preceded by an exclamation mark.

If you had wanted to sum cell B5 in the London, Dundee and Belfast sheets the formula would read **=SUM(London,Dundee,Belfast!B5)**.

This formula can now be copied to the remaining cells in the plan.

7   Ensure cell B5 on the *Totals* sheet is the active cell.

8   Click on the *Copy* button.

9   Select the range B6:B10

10   Select *Edit | Paste |Special* and click on the *Formula* option. Click *OK*.

If you had just pasted as opposed to using the *Paste Special* command the formatting applied to cell B5 would be copied through the range and you would lose the borders and the currency formatting on the totals.

You can now copy the range B5:B10 to C5:F10 using the Paste command as you want to copy the formatting from the source cells.

11   Select the range B5.B10 if it is not already highlighted.

12   Click on the *Copy* button.

13   Select the range C5:F10 and click on the *Paste* button.

Note: *You could also use AutoFill to perform the second half of the above copy*.

Figure 6.3 shows the completed *Totals* sheet.

Figure 6.3. Completed Totals sheet

	A	B	C	D	E	F
1	TRENDY TOYS					
2	National Quarterly Sales Forecast					
3						
4		January	February	March	April	Quarterly Total
5	Baby & Toddler	7030	7096	7162	7230	28518
6	Educational	6830	6893	6957	7021	27700
7	Dolls	7500	7571	7642	7714	30428
8	Models	5650	5703	5756	5809	22917
9	Garden	5550	5603	5656	5710	22519
10	Total Monthly Sales	£ 32,560	£ 32,865	£ 33,173	£ 33,484	£ 132,081
11						

Working with Multiple Workbooks

Sometimes you will want to keep information in separate workbook files, but pick up certain data in one file for use in another. For example, you could take the Total Monthly Sales from the Trendy Toys sales forecast and use them in a Profit and Loss account.

A very simple profit and loss account will be created to demonstrate how cells can be referenced and linked between different Excel workbook files.

1   With the TRENDY_N workbook still open, create a new workbook by clicking on the *New* button.

2   Enter titles and formatting as shown in Figure 6.4. The plan has been formatted using the Classic 1 option in AutoFormat.

Figure 6.4.
Titles for the profit
and loss account

	A	B	C	D	E	F
1			Trendy Toys			
2			Quarterly Profit and Loss			
3						
4		January	February	March	April	Total
5	Sales					
6	Fixed Costs					
7	Direct Costs					
8	Gross Profit					
9						

3   Save this plan as TREND_PL.

4   Click in cell B5.

5   Type =

6   You want to pick up the total sales figure for January from the *Totals* sheet of TRENDY_N.

7   Select the *Window* command and TRENDY_N will be listed as one of the open windows. Click on the file reference to switch to that window.

8   Click on cell B10.

9   The formula bar now reads =**[TRENDY_N.XLS]Totals!$B$10**

10   Press ENTER to complete the formula and you will automatically return to the profit and loss plan.

This formula can be interpreted as taking the contents of cell B10 in the *Totals* sheet of the file TRENDY_N.XLS.

When referencing cells in other workbooks you must always reference the filename first together with the full path if it is not in the same directory, and the name must be enclosed in square brackets ([ ]). The sheet reference follows (in a single sheet workbook this is likely to be *Sheet 1*), and the cell reference or references are preceded by an exclamation mark (!).

This formula should be copied to the range C5:E5, but before this can be done an adjustment to the B10 reference must be made. When you reference cells in another file using the mouse, Excel will always make the reference *absolute*. This is indicated by the dollar signs ($) that precede the column and row references and means that if the formula is copied anywhere the reference to cell B10 will remain fixed. In this example the reference should be relative so that when the formula is copied it will adjust to being C10, D10 etc. The reference can easily be changed using the F4 function key.

11 Ensure cell B5 in the profit and loss plan is the active cell and press F2 to edit the contents.

12 Position the insertion point somewhere on the $B$5 reference and each time you press F4 the reference will change between absolute ($B$10), mixed ($B10 or B$10) and relative (B10). When the reference is relative press ENTER. The formula now reads:

=SUM([TRENDY_N.XLS]Totals!B10).

(Absolute references are covered in more detail in Chapter Eight).

This formula can now be copied to the range C5:E5.

13 With cell B5 as the active cell, use *AutoFill* to copy the formula to cell E5.

Click on cell D5 and the formula bar reads

SUM([TRENDY_N.XLS]Totals!D10).

which is picking up the Total sales for March on the *Totals* sheet of the TRENDY_N file.

Note: *You can type in a formula that references other sheets or other files instead of using the mouse, but it is important to ensure that the references are absolutely correct.*

Complete the Plan

1   Click in cell B6 and type **10000.**

2   Click in cell C6 and reference B6 as the fixed costs will not change, **=B6.**

3   Use *AutoFill* to copy the reference to cell E6.

4   Click in cell C7 and enter a formula for directs costs to be 30% of sales: **=B5*.30.**

5   Use *AutoFill* to copy the formula to cell E7.

6   Click in cell F5 where the total sales are required.

7   Click the *AutoSum* button.

Even though you have not specified a range to sum, AutoSum has guessed. You can accept its suggestion either by pressing ENTER or by clicking the tick on the Formula Bar.

Note: *If the suggestion was not correct, click and drag the range you want to sum.*

8   Use *AutoFill* to copy the totals down to cell F7.

9   Enter a formula for the Gross Profit in cell B8 as **=B5-B6-B7.**

10   Use *AutoFill* to copy the formula to cell F8.

11   Update the plan on disk by clicking on the *Save* button 🖫.

Figure 6.5 shows the completed profit and loss plan.

*Figure 6.5.
Completed Profit
and Loss Plan*

	A	B	C	D	E	F
1		TRENDY TOYS				
2		National Quarterly Sales Forecast				
3						
4		January	February	March	April	Quarterly Total
5	Baby & Toddler	7030	7096	7162	7230	£ 28,518
6	Educational	6830	6893	6957	7021	£ 27,700
7	Dolls	7500	7571	7642	7714	£ 30,428
8	Models	5650	5703	5756	5809	£ 22,917
9	Garden	5550	5603	5656	5710	£ 22,519
10	Total Monthly Sales	£ 32,560	£ 32,865	£ 33,173	£ 33,484	£ 132,081

Before continuing close all open workbooks, saving any updates if necessary.

Updating Links

When you come to use workbooks that contain links to other workbooks the links can automatically be updated when you open the file.

1   Open TRENDY_N.XLS and change the Baby and Toddler sales for January to zero.

2   Save and close the file.

Tip: *You can Close the file without saving it first as Excel will detect that changes have been made and will ask you if you want to update the file before closing.*

3   Open TREND_PL.XLS and the message shown in Figure 6.6 will be displayed on the screen.

*Figure 6.6.
Update links
message screen.*

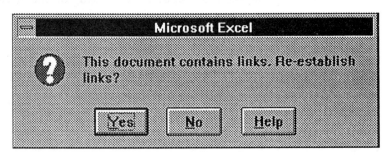

4   If you choose *No* the file will be opened with the last values it was previously saved with.

5   Select *Yes* and the links will be updated.

          Note: *If you choose not to update the links, but at a later stage want to so do you can select Edit | Links and then choose Update Now from the dialogue box.*

          If you have both the profit and loss account and the national forecast files open at the same time the links will automatically be updated each the source file is recalculated.

Summary

This chapter has introduced you to some of the more powerful file handling features of Excel. By modularising applications into small manageable sections through the use of multiple sheets and linked files you can keep better control of your system. It is important to bear in mind, however, that if you link multiple large files you must have adequate hardware to backup the power given to you by Excel.

Self Test

1   What sheet types does Excel recognise as part of a workbook?

2   How do you change the sheet tab label?

3   How do you group a series of sheets?

4   What tasks can be performed whilst sheets are grouped?

5   How do you ungroup sheets?

6   How do you display multiple sheets on the screen together?

7   What is the format of a cell reference that references a cell in another sheet in the same workbook?

8   What is the format of a cell reference that references a cell in a sheet in another workbook?

9   What happens if you close a file without saving it first?

10   What happens when you open a workbook that contains links to another file?

SEVEN
Working with Charts

Key Learning Points in this Chapter

- Creating charts with the Chart Wizard

- Embedded charts vs chart sheets

- Changing chart types

- Formatting charts

- Adding, deleting and changing chart data

Introduction

Effective and meaningful presentation of data is extremely important when attempting to communicate information. In a spreadsheet, the data may either be presented numerically, i.e. in a tabular format, or graphically. The power of graphical presentation of data is well known, but has always been either difficult, very time consuming or both to achieve. Graphing in Excel has always been straightforward, and with the introduction of the *Chart Wizard* in Excel 4, the time spent in producing them was significantly reduced. In Excel 5, the charting engine has received a major overhaul resulting in a simplified interface for creating, modifying and customising charts. New features include the facility to drag and drop data into a chart in order to add a data point or data series, error bars and trendlines, and flexible combination charts. The charting engine is thus a very powerful tool which is at the same time flexible and easy to use.

The first exercise will be to create a simple chart using the *Chart Wizard* to show its speed and power. A more complex example will then be developed going through the process in more detail. This will include changing the type of chart, the formatting and modifying the chart data. Only the basics of charting will be covered, but having completed this chapter, you will be in a position to experiment with the facilities provided.

The Chart Wizard

Central to the concept of quickly and easily creating charts is *the Chart Wizard*. Step by step, you are lead through the creation of a chart, with the *Chart Wizard* suggesting various alternatives.

A graph will be created showing the national sales forecast figures for the months of January through March for each of the different product categories.

1   Open the file TRENDY_N and save it as TRENDY_G.

2   Select the range A4:E9.

3 Click the Chart Wizard tool ⬚ on the Standard toolbar.

4 Press PGDN to make room for the graph.

5 The mouse pointer has changed to a cross with a graph image bedside it. Position it on the worksheet where you want the top left-hand corner of the chart to be. Click and drag the pointer in the sheet to produce a box into which the graph will be placed. The exact size doesn't matter but use most of the screen space.

6 Release the mouse button and the Chart Wizard dialogue box is displayed as shown in Figure 7.1. Check that the range is correct.

7 Click the *Finish* button.

Figure 7.1.
The Chart Wizard
Dialog box.

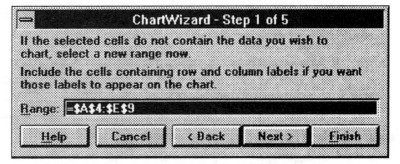

Excel interprets the data and produces the chart shown in Figure 7.2.

Figure 7.2.
Default chart
created with the
Chart Wizard
settings.

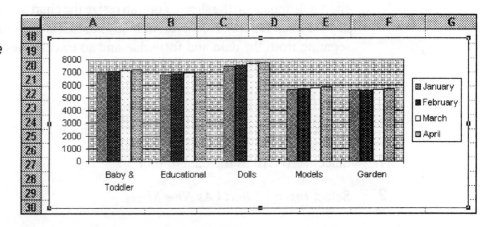

Note: *If all the names along the X-axis do not appear, press* DEL *to remove the graph and repeat the steps above, making the plot area larger.*

Charts are by default linked to the worksheet cells. In other words, when any data on the worksheet is changed, this is reflected on the graph. For example, to see what the effect of removing dolls from the London branch would have on the National Quarterly Sales Forecast:

1   Go to the *London* spreadsheet by clicking on the tab.

2   Type **0** into cell B7.

3   Return to the *Total* spreadsheet and observe the effect of the change on the graph.

4   Go back to the *London* spreadsheet and change B7 back to 3000.

Exercise

> **1**   On the London sheet of TRENDY_G create a graph showing the Total Quarterly Sales.

Embedded charts Vs Chart sheets

The chart you have just created is an example of an *embedded* chart. These are charts that are part of a worksheet, and when you print the worksheet, the chart will appear on the sheet. You can resize the chart and incorporate as part of your main reports. However, in many cases it is preferable to keep charts separate from the data and formulae and so Excel gives you the option of using a *Chart Sheet*.

Chart Sheets

To create a chart of the Total Quarterly Sales using a chart sheet:

1   Select A10:E10 as the data to plot.

2   Select *Insert | Chart | As New Sheet*.

3 In the Chart Wizard dialogue box, click the *Finish* button.

A chart of the total monthly sales is produced on a separate sheet called Chart 1. A tab label has been added to the list at the bottom of the screen. The graph may be seen in Figure 7.3.

Figure 7.3. Creating a chart using a chart sheet.

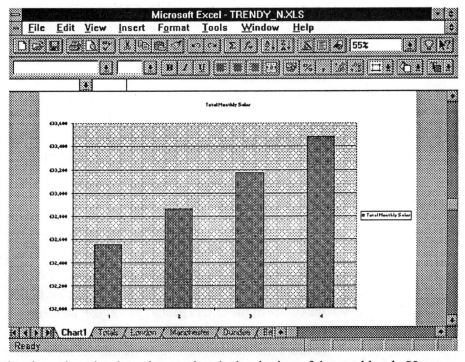

The chart sheet has been inserted at the beginning of the workbook. You can move it to a different location by clicking on the tab label and dragging the mouse pointer across the tabs to the required location.

Note: *There is a shortcut to creating a chart sheet using the default Excel chart: Select the data you want to plot and then press F11.*

If you want to delete the chart sheet:

1 Make sure you are currently in that sheet, and then select *Edit | Delete Sheet*.

2 Select *OK* when asked to continue.

Exercise

---
1   Create a chart using a chart sheet showing the quarterly sales of
         each product in Dundee.

Activating Vs Selecting an Embedded Chart

This section applies to any object embedded in a worksheet, e.g. text boxes, pictures or charts. When dealing with embedded objects, it is important to realise that they are positioned, as it were, on top of the worksheet. This may be seen by changing the active cell, using the arrow keys, under the object and out the other side. Thus a distinction must be made between when the object is to be moved about or resized, and when the object itself is to be edited. This distinction is made through either *selecting* or *activating* the object.

Selecting Objects

To select an object, click on it**once**. You will notice that there are eight small squares, or handles, which appear at the corners and in the middle of each side, as in Figure 7.2 above. These handles may be used to alter the size of the object. Place the mouse pointer over one of handles and notice that it changes into a double headed arrow. Click and drag the handle towards or away from the centre of the object to change its size. Resizing an object using one of the corner handles retains its perspective, whereas using the other handles reduces the size but can make the object look distorted when it is printed.

Deleting an object is simply a case of selecting that object and then pressing the DEL key.

Activating Objects

To activate an object, **double click** on it, and a thick border will appear around the outside as shown in Figure 7.4. This will enable you to edit the object, in this case, the chart itself. Double clicking on any of the components within the graph will enable you to change them as you see fit. The drop-down menus have changed to include the various charting options.

Figure 7.4.
An activated
chart.

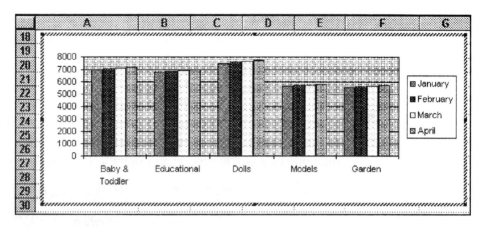

Data Series and Data Points

Before going any further, the distinction must be made between a data series and a data point. A *data point* is a single point on a graph that has a specific value. For example, in Figure 7.4 cell B5 is the January value for Baby and Toddler. A *data series* represents a single row or column of data and is made up of related data points. Each series is distinguished by a unique colour or pattern, for example, cells B5:B9 is the data series for the January data.

Further Features of the Chart Wizard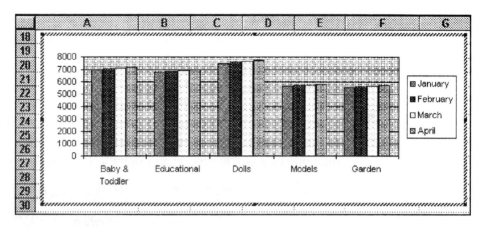

In the previous examples the default options of the Chart Wizard where used by immediately clicking on the *Finish* button, which skipped over most of the Chart Wizard's options. Here, we will examine each of the steps in more detail.

For this example, a chart will be created showing the sales forecasts on the Model and Garden product categories for Manchester and Dundee.

1 Go to the Manchester chart by clicking on the tab at the bottom of the page.

2 Select the cells A4:E4. It is very important that you include A4 even though it is empty.

3 Hold down the CTRL key, and using the mouse pointer, select the cells

A8:E9. Do not let go of the CTRL key until you have finished the selection. This is how you can select a set of non-adjacent cells in a worksheet.

4   Check that the cells A4:E4 as well as the cells A8:E9 are selected. If not, start again from step 2.

5   Click on the *Chart Wizard* button, move down to make space for the graph and draw a box as you did in the first exercise. The Chart Wizard dialogue box will appear as in Figure 7.3. Check the ranges are correct.

*Figure 7.5.
The Chart Wizard
Dialog box.*

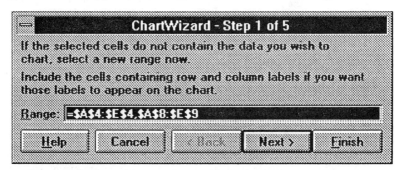

The five buttons on the dialogue box have the following functions:

*   Help - Gives you help on the 5 steps of the Chart Wizard

*   Cancel - Stops the process of creating a chart. No chart is created.

*   Back - Takes you back one step. This option is not available on this step as it is the first step.

*   Next - Takes you to the next step.

*   Finish - When you are finished specifying chart properties, click on this button to create the chart.

6   Click on the *Next* button.

7   The dialogue box for Step 2 of 5 is displayed as shown in Figure 7.6 where you may select a chart type. The Chart Wizard has suggested the Column type. This is what we want, so click on the *Next* button.

Figure 7.6.
Chart Wizard -
Choose the type
of chart you want.

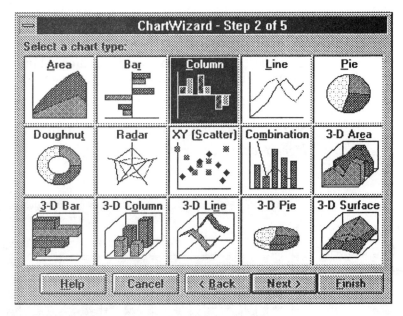

8 The dialogue box for Step 3 of 5 is displayed as shown in Figure 7.7.
Here, you may select a format for the chart type you have selected. Again,
we will remain with the suggestion of format 6. Click on the *Next* button.

Figure 7.7.
Chart Wizard -
Selecting a chart
format.

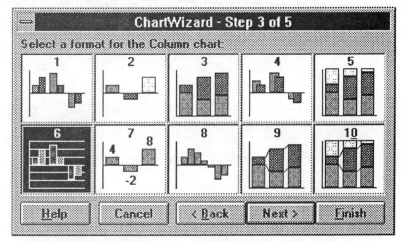

9 The dialogue box for Step 4 of 5 is displayed as shown in Figure 7.8. The
orientation of the chart is specified here, i.e. whether the data series are in
rows or columns. For this graph, the data series is in rows, the first being

used for the category (X) axis labels and the first column for legend text
so the suggested settings are correct.

You may specify how many rows and/or columns contain text to be used for
labels and legend entries. When you specify zero, the first row or column is
displayed as a data series or data points.

Note: *You may select multiple rows and/or columns for X-axis labels and
legend text since Excel is capable of charting multi-level categories.*

*Figure 7.8.
Chart Wizard -
Selecting a chart
format.*

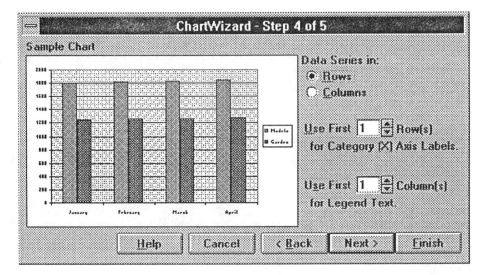

10   The final Chart Wizard dialogue box for Step 5 of 5 is displayed as shown
in Figure 7.9.

11   Fill in the chart title and Y axis title as shown.

Figure 7.9.
Chart Wizard -
Selecting chart
and axis titles and
a legend display.

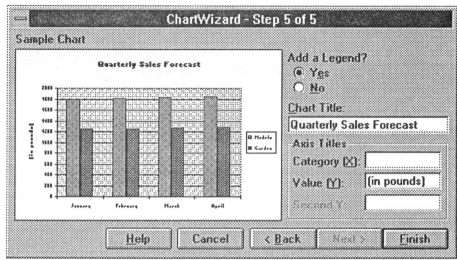

12   Click *Finish* to create the chart shown in Figure 7.10.

At this point the chart only reflects the sales forecast for models and garden products in Manchester

Figure 7.10.
Chart showing
sales forecast
figures of Models
and Garden
product
categories for
Manchester only.

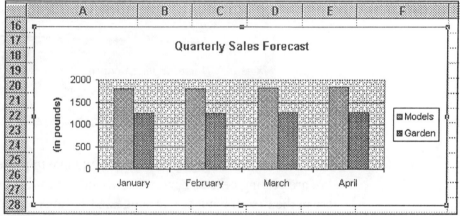

Adding New Data to a Chart

1   To include the additional data for Dundee, click on the Dundee tab

2   Cells A8 and A9 will form the legend and in order to differentiate between Dundee and Manchester double click on cell A8 to edit it and type in "(Dundee)" after "Models". Do the same for cell A9.

3   Select cells A8:E9 as shown in Figure 7.11.

Figure 7.11
Data for the chart
from the Dundee
sheet.

7	Dolls	1400	1417	1434	1451	£
8	Models (Dundee)	1450	1467	1485	1503	£
9	Garden (Dundee)	1350	1366	1383	1399	£
10	Total Monthly Sales	£ 6,800	£ 6,882	£ 6,964	£ 7,048	£
11						

4   Copy the selected cells using the *Copy* button or *Edit | Copy*,

5   Return to the Manchester spreadsheet. Activate the chart by double
clicking on it - make sure it is activated and not just selected

6   Select *Edit | Paste Special...* which will give you a dialogue box as in
Figure 7.12.

Figure 7.12.
Pasting in charts.

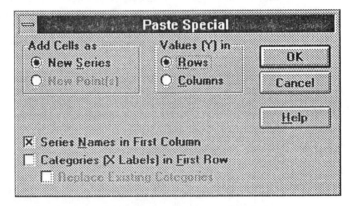

This allows you to specify how you would like to paste new data to a chart.
We are pasting cells as new series, which appear in rows. The series names
are in the first column so the suggested settings are correct.

7   Click on the *OK* button, which will give you the chart shown in Figure
7.13.

Note: *If you would like Manchester to appear in brackets after the top two*
series in the legend, then edit cells A8 and A9 in the worksheet as you did for
Dundee.

*Figure 7.13.
Chart showing
sales forecast
figures of Models
and Garden
product
categories for
Manchester and
Dundee.*

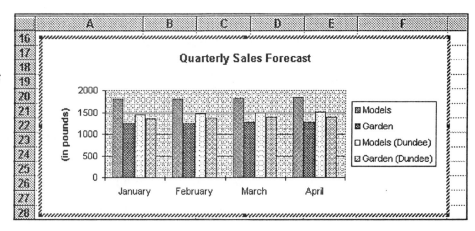

Formatting Charts

You can now create charts from data in a spreadsheet. Customising your charts to display the information in the most appropriate way is just as important. Figure 7.14 illustrates the different chart elements.

*Figure 7.14.
Chart elements.*

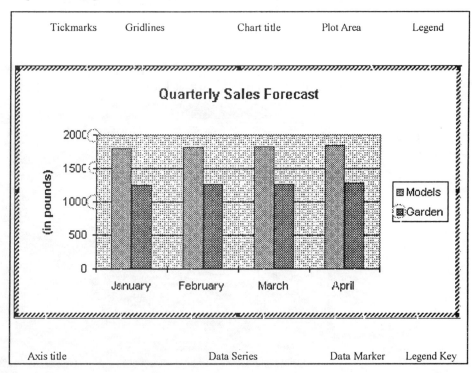

To edit a chart, it must first be activated. This is achieved by double clicking on it if it is an embedded chart, or by clicking on the tab label if it is a chart sheet.

There are three ways of accessing the elements of a chart once it has been activated:

- Click once on the element and select from the pull-down menus to format it.

- Double click on the element to directly access the formatting options.

- Right click on the element and select one of the options from the shortcut menu.

To print the chart in Figure 7.13 it would be preferable to take out the shading, and perhaps the gridlines. We will also put on some data labels for emphasis and change the legend slightly.

Removing Chart Shading and Borders

1   Activate the chart.

2   Double click somewhere on the grey shaded area of the chart - the plot area to produce the Format Plot Area dialogue box shown in Figure 7.15.

Figure 7.15. Formatting the Plot Area.

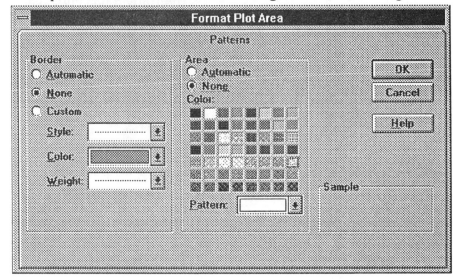

3   Change the *Border* to *None* and the *Area* to *None*.

4   Click on the *OK* button to return to the chart.

Note: *This is how you set the border and/or the fill area of any of the other elements. Select the element, click on the patterns tab and change the Border and Area options to what you require.*

Removing Gridlines

1   Right click with the mouse pointer on one of the gridlines.

2   Select *Insert Gridlines*.

3   Click on *Major Gridlines* under *Value (Y) Axis*.

4   Clear all boxes as shown in Figure 7.16.

5   Click *OK* to return to the chart.

Figure 7.16.
The Gridlines
Dialogue Box.

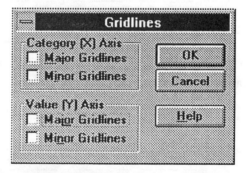

Moving the Chart Legend

1   Double click on the chart legend.

2   To change the placement of the legend, click on the *Placement* tab at the top right of the Format Legend dialogue box shown in Figure 7.17.

3   Change the type to *Bottom*.

4   To change the font, border or fill area, select the appropriate tab at the top of the screen and change it to suit you.

Figure 7.17.
The Format
Legend dialogue
box.

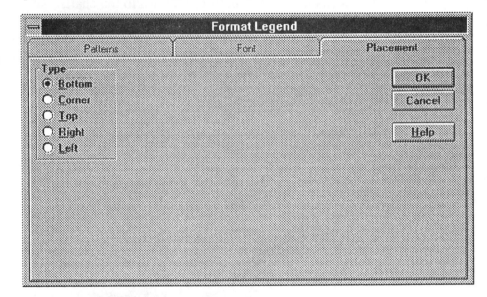

Inserting Data Labels

1   To insert a data label, right click on one of the series - *Models* for example, and select ***Insert Data Labels...*** from the short-cut menu.

2   In the dialogue box shown in Figure 7.18 select the *Show Value* option.

3   Click on the *OK* button to return to the chart.

Figure 7.18.
Data Labels.

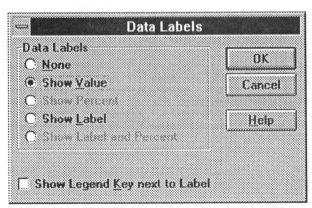

Formatting Data Labels

1   Right click on one of the Data labels.

2   Select the ***Format Data Label...*** option.

3   Click on the *Font* tab and change the font to something different to the current font.

4   Click on the *Number* tab and change the number to currency format.

5   Click on the *OK* button.

Formatting the Chart Object

1   To complete the chart, the chart object itself can be formatted.

2   Click on the spreadsheet to deactivate the chart.

3   Right-click on the chart.

4   Select ***Format Object*** from the short-cut menu.

5   Click on the *Properties* tab at the top of the dialogue box.

6   Change the thickness of the border and click on the *Round Corners* check-box.

7   Click on the *OK* button to return to the chart which now appears as shown in Figure 7.19. (Objects are covered in more detail in Chapter Twelve).

Note: *On previous versions of Excel it was not possible to place graphical objects (boxes, circles, lines, text boxes, etc...) on charts - this restriction has now been removed.*

Figure 7.19.
The completed
chart.

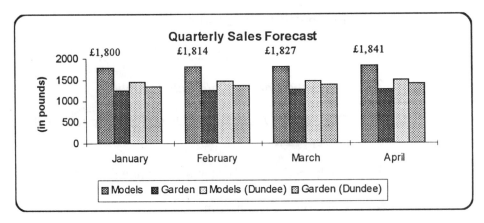

Exercise

1   Add a text box saying "Note difference" to the graph you have just created (Fig 7.18) with two arrows pointing to the Garden forecast for both Manchester and Dundee in April.

Modifying chart data

There are basically three ways in which you can modify chart data: you can add to it, you can delete or remove unwanted information or you can reorganise it.

Adding data to a chart

Earlier, you copied data from the Dundee worksheet and pasted it onto the chart with the Manchester data. Data can be added to a chart in this way from any sheet or workbook that is open.

When data is being added from the same sheet, you can drag and drop the data into the chart without the chart being selected or activated. For example to add the data for Dolls in Manchester to the chart:

1   Select the range A7:E7.

2   Move the mouse pointer to the outside edge of the selected range and when the pointer changes from a cross into an arrow, drag the block into the chart and release the button.

3   Click *OK* to accept the settings in the dialogue box and the chart is updated.

With the chart activated, you can use the Insert menu to add data from the sheet you are working in, or any other sheet or workbook that is open at that time. To add the Baby & Toddler data for Manchester to the chart:

1   Select *Insert | New Data*.

2   Click on the Manchester sheet if it is not the active sheet.

3   Select the range B5:E5 (you will see the range appearing in the dialogue box).

4   Click the *OK* button and the chart is updated with the new data.

Deleting data from a chart

You can either delete an entire data series or you can choose to delete specific data points. To delete the Baby & Toddler data series just added:

1   Activate the chart.

2   Click somewhere on the series and press the DEL key.

3   You can also right click on the series and select *Clear*.

To remove a data point you must remove the data from the worksheet or change the range plotted in the chart. For example, to remove the February data in the Dolls series:

1   Click somewhere on the worksheet to ensure the chart is de-activated.

2   Delete cell C7 of the plan which will set the remaining periods to zero.

3   Edit cell D7 to read =**B7*1.01**.

The chart has changed and the Dolls data point for February is no longer there.

Manually Reorganising Chart Data

Finally, when the chart is activated, a single click will allow you to edit the series manually through the formula bar. Figure 7.20 shows the different parts of a data series reference when it is displayed in the formula bar.

Figure 7.20. Manually editing the data series in the formula bar.

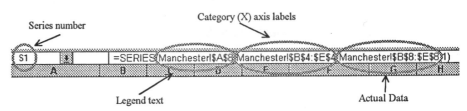

If you double click on the series, and choose the *Name and Values* tab in the dialogue box shown in Figure 7.21, you may change the selected data series and the legend text.

Figure 7.21. Changing a data series using the Format Data Series dialogue box.

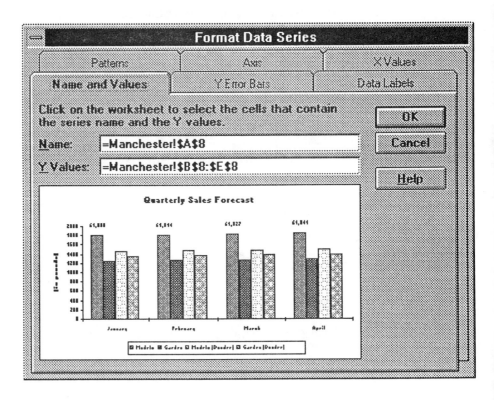

Tip: *It is now possible to use pictures to represent data series. To find out more about this facility use the Search function in the Help system. Type in "pictures, replacing data markers with".*

Exercise

1   Close any existing workbooks. Open TRENDY_N and save it as TREND_GX.

2   Create a chart showing the total monthly sales forecast figures for each month for London, Manchester, Dundee and Belfast. Change the chart type to 3-D Column and change the series order so all of them are visible.

Summary

The Chart Wizard is integral in making Excel's charting facilities easy to use. It involves a five step process where the series is checked, the chart type selected, the format specified, the orientation corrected and titles and legends added.

A chart may either appear embedded as an integral part of a or as a sheet on its own. Care must be taken when working with embedded charts as they can be either selected or activated and the functions available are different depending on the status of the chart.

Formatting chart elements can be achieved either by selecting the element and using the menus, by double clicking on the element which will bring up the formatting dialogue box, or by right clicking on the element and selecting the appropriate action from the short-cut menu.

Self Test

1   If you change the data from which the graph was created, will the chart reflect the changes made?

2   What is the difference between activating and selecting a chart?

3   Can you change the format of a data series when a chart is selected?

4   What is a data series as opposed to a data point? How do you select a data point in a chart?

5   Can you draw three dimensional charts in Excel and in which step of the Chart Wizard would you select this option?

6   How can you add a legend and titles to a chart after you have completed step 5 of the Chart Wizard?

7   What are the different ways of adding new data to a chart?

8   What are tickmarks and gridlines?

9   How would you add a data label to a data point?

10   How would you remove a data point from a graph?

EIGHT
What-If Analysis

Key Learning Points In This Chapter

- Changing opening assumptions
- Using absolute addresses and range names for greater control
- Data tables for what-if analysis

Introduction

What-if analysis may be defined as the process of changing assumptions in a plan in order to see the effect of such changes on the objectives. It is a direct product of the fact that once a plan has been entered into the computer it may be recalculated again and again at electronic speeds. Thus you can change input data or input relationships and immediately recalculate the worksheet to see the impact of these changes on critical output factors.

A typical what-if type question might be to ask what effect a 2% increase in direct labour costs will have on profit and return on investment, or what effect will a further 30 day delay in receiving cash from the debtors have on the overdraft and/or return on investment.

What-if questions may be put one at a time or several at once. If it is necessary to investigate the effect of two simultaneous changes in the assumptions it is usually advantageous to also consider these one at a time, so that the individual effects as well as the joint effects are known. Irrespective of whether single or multiple changes to input are made, multiple output will usually be monitored.

Excel provides for several different levels of what-if analysis. In the simplest case all that is required is to change the value of a data cell and the impact of the change will be seen as soon as the worksheet is recalculated. For more powerful what-if there are *data tables* which allow a series of what-if questions to be analysed at one time, producing a tabular report of the possible results.

Simple What-If Analysis

For even the simplest what-if analysis to be successful it is necessary for a plan to have been carefully constructed with correct relationships and logic.

1   Open TRENDY_N and save the file as TRENDY_W.

2   Click on the *London* tab.

3   Change the Baby and Toddler opening sales to **1000**.

The worksheet is immediately recalculated as can be seen in Figure 8.1.

Figure 8.1. Changing an opening assumption.

	A	B	C	D	E	F
1		TRENDY TOYS - London Branch				
2		Quarterly Sales Forecast				
3						
4		January	February	March	April	Quarterly Total
5	Baby & Toddler	1000	1010	1020	1030	£ 4,060
6	Educational	2100	2121	2142	2164	£ 8,527
7	Dolls	3000	3030	3060	3091	£ 12,181
8	Models	1200	1212	1224	1236	£ 4,872
9	Garden	1800	1818	1836	1855	£ 7,309
10	Total Monthly Sales	£ 9,100	£ 9,191	£ 9,283	£ 9,376	£ 36,950

In fact it is not just the current worksheet that is recalculated, but the entire workbook.

4   Click on the *Totals* tab and notice how the figures here have also changed to reflect the reduction in sales.

Note: *If you are working with a large plan and have set recalculation to manual (Tools | Options | Manual) then you will have to press F9 to see the effect of the change.*

If you want to change the growth rate for Baby and Toddler sales in London you have to edit the formula in cell C5 and copy it to the remaining periods. This illustrates how embedding growth rates and other factors in formulae makes changing values more difficult than if they were located elsewhere on the worksheet.

Extracting Embedded Factors

The design of the Trendy Toys forecast could be changed so that there will no longer be embedded factors in the plan.

The first step is to allocate a separate area into which the factors may be placed. With a large model it would be sensible to put all the input factors etc., on a separate sheet, but for this example the growth rates will be placed below the main plan.

1   Click on the *London* tab.

2   Add the information shown in Figure 8.2 to the plan.

Figure 8.2.
Growth rates for
London.

	A	B	C	D	E	F
1		TRENDY TOYS - London Branch				
2		Quarterly Sales Forecast				
3						
4		January	February	March	April	Quarterly Total
5	Baby & Toddler	1000	1010	1020	1030	£ 4,060
6	Educational	2100	2121	2142	2164	£ 8,527
7	Dolls	3000	3030	3060	3091	£ 12,181
8	Models	1200	1212	1224	1236	£ 4,872
9	Garden	1800	1818	1836	1855	£ 7,309
10	Total Monthly Sales	£ 9,100	£ 9,191	£ 9,283	£ 9,376	£ 36,950
11						
12	Growth rates					
13	Baby & Toddler	1.00%				
14	Educational	1.50%				
15	Dolls	1.00%				
16	Models	0.90%				
17	Garden	1.05%				

Absolute Addresses

When a formula is copied in Excel the relationships in the formula are maintained. This is referred to as a *relative* copy. If you look at the Baby and Toddler row you can see that the formula in cell C6 takes the value in B6 and increases it by 1%. When the formula is copied a relative relationship is retained so that in column D the value in cell C6 is increased by 1%.

The formula in cell C5 has to be changed to refer to the growth rate in cell B13 and it would be quite acceptable to enter =B5*B13. However, when this formula is copied to cells D5 and E5 incorrect results will be returned because the reference to cell B13 will change to reference cell C13 and D13, which are blank.

To solve the problem you can make an *absolute* reference to cell B13 by preceding the column and row reference with a dollar sign ($). Now when the formula is copied the reference to cell B5 will change to C5, D5 etc., but the reference to cell B13 remains fixed.

1   C5=B5*(1+$B$13)

2   Drag the fill handle across to extend the formula to E5.

3   Repeat the above two steps for the other product categories.

Tip: *Instead of typing in the dollar signs you can type the cell reference and with the insertion point anywhere on the cell reference, or immediately after it, press F4.*

You may find there are occasions when you need to fix only the row or the column part of cell reference. You can do this by preceding only the row or the column with the dollar sign. For example, B$13 will fix only the row and $B13 fixes only the column.

Figure 8.3 shows the formulae for some of the plan after the changes have been made.

Figure 8.3. Amended formulae incorporating absolute references.

	A	B	C	D
3				
4		January	February	March
5	Baby & Toddler	1000	=B5*(1+$B$13)	=C5*(1+$B$13)
6	Educational	2100	=B6*(1+$B$14)	=C6*(1+$B$14)
7	Dolls	3000	=B7*(1+$B$15)	=C7*(1+$B$15)
8	Models	1200	=B8*(1+$B$16)	=C8*(1+$B$16)
9	Garden	1800	=B9*(1+$B$17)	=C9*(1+$B$17)
10	Total Monthly Sales	=SUM(B5:B9)	=SUM(C5:C9)	=SUM(D5:D9)

To perform what-if analysis on the growth rates is now just a case of changing the values in the range B13:B19. The added benefit of having this data in a separate area is that you can quickly see what the growth rates are without having to select a cell and look at the formula bar.

Exercise

1   Amend the other regional offices in the TRENDY_W file so that the growth rates are displayed in the same way as they now are for London.

Data Tables for What-If Analysis

Regardless of whether it is the opening values or the factors that require analysis, if a large number of changes are required in order to establish the most sensitive variable, or the most appropriate value, the individual changing of the data can be a lengthy process.

Excel provides a feature whereby a range of data for a particular input variable or variables may be entered into a separate part of the worksheet, and this data may then be compared against one or more output variables in the plan. For example, in order to ascertain the most profitable volume level a range of different opening volumes may be entered into the worksheet and the effect of each of these be seen on the Net Profit for January, July and December. The command used to perform this type of analysis is *Data | Table*.

There are two basic types of data table, a one-way and a two-way table.

A one-way table allows one input factor to be analysed against as many output variables as you require. With a two-way table there are two input factors, and a single output variable.

One-Way Data Tables

A one-way data table can be created to look at varying opening volumes for the Baby and Toddler sales for London. Volumes between 950 and 1500 will be considered.

1   Ensure you are in the *London* sheet

2   Enter the information shown in Figure 8.4.

3   C21 =**F5**

F5 is the Quarterly total sales for the Baby and Toddler category and we are interested in seeing how this is affected by changing the opening sales.

Figure 8.4.
Setting up a one-
way data table.

	A	B	C	D	E
18					
19		What if analysis on opening volumes			
20		for Baby and Toddler			
21		£ 4,060			
22		950			
23		975			
24		1000			
25		1250			
26		1500			

4   Select the area **B21:C26.**

5   Select *Data | Table*

The dialogue box in Figure 8.5 is displayed.

Figure 8.5.
Data table
dialogue box.

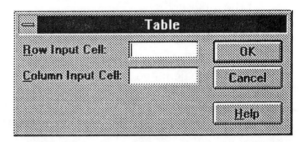

As this is a 1-way table you only need to complete the *Column Input Cell*. This refers to the cell in the main plan that you want to replace with the values in the column of the table.

Tip: *If a dialogue box obstructs the part of the worksheet you want to look at you can click on the title bar and drag it elsewhere on the screen.*

6   Click in the *Column Input Cell* box

7   Click on cell B5

8   Click *OK*

The table is immediately calculated and the results are displayed as shown in Figure 8.6.

Figure 8.6.
Completed data-
table.

	A	B	C	D	E
19		What if analysis on opening volumes			
20		for Baby and Toddler			
21			£ 4,060		
22		950	3857.38		
23		975	3958.89		
24		1000	4060.4		
25		1250	5075.5		
26		1500	6090.6		

When you click *OK* in the Data Table dialogue box Excel takes the first value in the input range (950) and puts it in the specified input cell (B5). The worksheet is recalculated and the result placed in cell C22. This process is repeated for all the cells in the input range. Only when all the calculation is complete is the table displayed and you never actually see the values changing in the input cell.

To test the accuracy of the table enter 975, for example, into cell B5 and notice that the Quarterly Total is £3959 - which with rounding is the same as the result calculated by the table.

There is no limit to the number of output cells that you can include in a one-way table, providing that there is a link between the input variable and the output cell.

For example it might be useful to have a table that looks at the effect of varying the growth rate for Baby and Toddler on the Quarterly Total and the overall total sales.

1   Set up the table as shown in Figure 8.7.

Tip: *Enter the growth rates as 1% etc. and then use the increase decimal button* to *display all the entries with the same number of decimal places.*

Figure 8.7.
Data table with
multiple output
cells.

	A	B	C	D	E
28		What if analysis on growth rates			
29		for Baby and Toddler			
30			£ 4,060	£ 37,012	
31		0.50%			
32		0.75%			
33		1.00%			
34		1.25%			
35		1.50%			

2   Enter the following references into C30 and D30.

C30   **=F5**

E30   **=F10**

3   Select the B30:D35 as the table range.

4   Select *Data | Table*

5   Click on the *Column Input Cell* box.

6   Click on cell B13.

7   Click *OK*.

The table is calculated and appears as shown in Figure 8.8.

Figure 8.8.
Completed data
table with multiple
output cells.

	A	B	C	D	E
28		What if analysis on growth rates			
29		for Baby and Toddler			
30			£ 4,060	£ 37,012	
31		0.50%	4030.1	36981.59	
32		0.75%	4045.23	36996.71	
33		1.00%	4060.4	37011.89	
34		1.25%	4075.63	37027.11	
35		1.50%	4090.9	37042.39	

Exercise

> **1** Create a data table on the Manchester sheet to analyse the effect
> on the Total Quarterly sales and the overall total sales of
> changing the opening value of Garden toys.

Two-Way Data Tables

Both the above tables have only had one input variable, but it is possible to
create a table with two input variables.

In the previous examples you saw the effect of changing the opening sales
value for Baby and Toddler and you, separately, saw the effect of changing
the growth rate. A two-way table will now be created to see the effect of
changing both these variables together.

1   Set up the table as shown in Figure 8.9.

*Figure 8.9.
Setting up a two-
way data table.*

	A	B	C	D	E	F	G
37		What if analysis on growth rates					
38		and opening values for Baby and Toddler					
39		£ 4,060	950	975	1000	1250	1500
40		0.50%					
41		0.75%					
42		1.00%					
43		1.25%					
44		1.50%					

With a two-way table it is only possible to have one output cell and the
reference to this must be placed in the top left corner of the table as indicated
in Figure 8.9.

2   Enter =**F5** into cell B39.

3   Select the B39:G43 as the table range.

4   Select ***Data | Table***

5   Click on the *Row Input Cell* box.

6   Click on cell B5.

7 Click on the *Column Input Cell* box.

8 Click on cell B13.

9 Click *OK*.

The table is calculated and appears as shown in Figure 8.10.

*Figure 8.10.
Completed two-
way table.*

	A	B	C	D	E	F	G
37		What if analysis on growth rates					
38		and opening values for Baby and Toddler					
39		£ 4,060	950	975	1000	1250	1500
40		0.50%	3828.6	3929.348	4030.1	5037.6252	6045.15
41		0.75%	3842.96	3944.095	4045.225	5056.5318	6067.838
42		1.00%	3857.38	3958.891	4060.401	5075.5013	6090.602
43		1.25%	3871.85	3973.736	4075.627	5094.5337	6113.44
44		1.50%	3886.36	3988.631	4090.903	5113.6292	6136.355

When you click *OK* in the Data Table dialogue box Excel takes the first value
in the column input range (.50%) and the first value in the row input range
(950) and puts them in the specified input cells (B13 and B5 respectively).
The worksheet is recalculated and the result placed in cell C22. This process
is repeated for all the cells in the input range.

From this table you can see that a growth rate of .5% and an opening sales
of 1250 will give a Quarterly Total in excess of £5,000, £5037.6 in fact.

Recalculating and Changing Data Tables

If the calculation is set to automatic data tables will be recalculated automatically
along with the rest of the worksheet. This means that if you change a value
in the table, or in the plan the table is immediately updated.

Although this sounds useful, there can be two drawbacks. Firstly you will
often find that you need to create large tables and these can take quite a long
time to recalculate. If you have several tables on a worksheet and they are
recalculated every time you do anything it will slow you down considerably.
Secondly, having produced a table you might want to make changes to the
plan, but not change the results of your table.

To solve these problems Excel provides an option under ***Tools | Options | Calculation*** to put calculation on *Automatic Except Tables*. Figure 8.11 shows this dialogue box.

Figure 8.11. Calculation dialogue box.

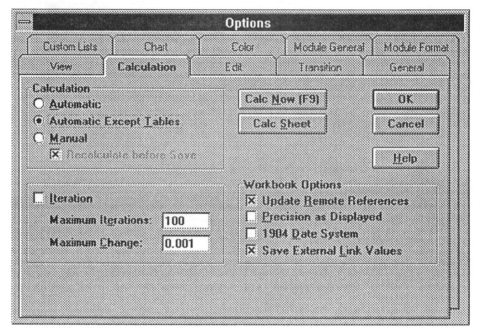

The results of a table are protected and if you attempt to overwrite or move anything an error message is displayed preventing you. You can, however, select all the results and delete them, should you need to.

Exercise

1   Create a data table on the Manchester sheet to analyse the effect on the overall total sales of changing the opening value and the growth rate of Garden toys.

Summary

What-if analysis, and data tables in particular is a powerful feature of Excel. Being able to perform multiple calculations quickly and display the results in an easy to read format means that a lot of analysis can be performed on your data.

Self Test

1   What constitutes an absolute cell reference and what are the options?

2   What function key can you use to make a cell reference absolute?

3   Why is it advantageous to display growth rates in a separate area of a plan as opposed to embedding them in a formula?

4   What is the difference between one-way and two-way data tables?

5   What must the range of a data table include?

6   Explain how a data table actually works

7   How can you test that the results of a data table are correct?

8   How can you prevent a table recalculating with the rest of the worksheet?

9   When deciding what to use as input and output variables what should you consider?

10   Can you change the data in a calculated data table?

NINE
Functions For Formula Development

Key Learning Points in this Chapter

- Overview of commonly required functions

- Incorporating functions into a plan

- Using the Function Wizard

- Incorporating logic using the IF functions

- Using LOOKUP functions

Introduction

Excel has several hundred built-functions which provide considerable power for manipulating text and numbers. These functions are broadly grouped in the following 11 categories:-

> Database and List
> Date and Time
> DDE and External
> Engineering
> Financial
> Information
> Logical
> Lookup and Reference
> Math and Trigonometry
> Statistical
> Text

A full listing can be obtained by listing functions by category from the Help Index.

A function can be used by itself, or can form part of a more complex formula. For example

$$=SUM(B2:B10)$$

is an example of the SUM function being used by itself and

$$=AVERAGE(B2:B8,INT(B13/B10),)*C10$$

is an example of a complex formula that incorporates two functions and some additional calculations.

Regardless of how many functions are incorporated in a formula and what function you are using there are some basic rules that must be followed:

- If the function is at the start of a formula it must be preceded by an equals sign (=), otherwise this is not necessary.

- The function name must be syntactically correct, for example AVG is not acceptable for the average function, it must be AVERAGE.

- Function names can be entered in upper or lower case, but Excel will convert the reference to upper case.

- Most functions require data on which to act, referred to as *arguments*. Arguments must be enclosed in parentheses following the function name. If there are multiple arguments each one is separated by a comma, for example =SUM(B10:B20,C10:C20).

- If a function does not require an argument it is referenced by the name followed by opening and closing parentheses. For example, =RAND().

Overview of Commonly Used Functions

In an introductory book such as this, it is not possible to give an in-depth coverage of Excel functions. However, knowing how to work with functions is extremely important and so in this chapter the following functions will be explained and put to use in practical examples:

> SUM
> AVERAGE
> ROUND
> INT
> MAX
> MIN
> ABS
> COUNT
> IF
> VLOOKUP
> HLOOKUP

The table of data in Figure 9.1 will initially be used as a basis for looking at the above functions. Type the numbers into a new workbook and save the file as FUNCTION.

Figure 9.1.
Function table.

	A	B	C	D	E
1		13	65	-60	6
2		1	200	-259	14
3		8	-9	5	7

The SUM Function

The SUM function returns the arithmetic total of all the specified arguments. SUM will total individual cells, a row, column, range or any combination of these, as well as actual values and results of formulae calculations. The following are valid examples of the uses of SUM:

=SUM(1,5.8,09,78)

=SUM(A1,B6,D8,H10)

=SUM(B2:M2)

=SUM(TURNOVER,B4,56)
(*where TURNOVER is an established range name*)

=SUM(B1*B2,100,B2:C4)

The SUM function will be used to create the totals of each column of the table in Figure 9.1.

1   A4   **SUM**

2   B4=**SUM(B1:B3)**

Note: *You can of course either type in or use the mouse to highlight the required range.*

Using AutoSum

Because the SUM function is so frequently required, there is a built-in feature in Excel called *AutoSum* which will automatically insert a SUM function for a specified range.

1   Click on cell C4 to make it the active cell.

2   Click on the

3   Excel decides on the most likely range that you intend to sum and displays it in the cell and on the Formula Bar. If the range is correct, which it is in this case, either press ENTER or click the tick button ▨ on the Formula Bar line to accept the formula.

4   With cell B7 still selected, drag the fill handle to extend the formula for the remaining columns. Figure 9.2 shows the results.

Figure 9.2.
Applying the SUM
function.

	A	B	C	D	E
1		13	65	-60	6
2		1	200	-259	14
3		8	-9	5	7
4	SUM	22	256	-314	27

If the suggested range was not the one you wanted you can either cancel the operation by clicking on the cross button ▨ on the Formula Bar or you can select the required range and then press ENTER which will replace the suggestion with your selection.

The AVERAGE Function

The AVERAGE function returns the average value of the cells specified. The arguments for an average function may be a row, column, range or any combination of these. In addition, constants and the result of formulae calculations may be incorporated.

When calculating the result, the AVERAGE function ignores blank cells and cells containing text. Thus, if a range is specified in which there are some text entries, an incorrect result will be returned. If a range to be averaged includes a blank you should replace the blank with a zero which will mean that cell will be included in the count. Figure 9.3 illustrates some of the pitfalls that can be encountered if the function is incorrectly applied.

Figure 9.3.
Potential
problems with the
AVERAGE
function.

	A	B	C
1	Sales	Sales	Sales
2	100	100	100
3	nil		0
4	200	200	200
5	=AVERAGE(A2:A4)	=AVERAGE(B2:B4)	=AVERAGE(C2:C4)

	A	B	C
1	Sales	Sales	Sales
2	100	100	100
3	nil		0
4	200	200	200
5	150	150	100

Valid examples of the average function are:-

=AVERAGE(4,6,89,65)

=AVERAGE(A1,54,GROWTH_RATE)

(where GROWTH_RATE is an established range name)

=AVERAGE(C1:R3)

=AVERAGE(A1:A4,C3:H4)

=AVERAGE(A4/B12,C3/H22)

The average of each column in the original table can be calculated as follows:-

1 A5 **Average**

2 B5=AVERAGE(B1:B3)

3 With cell B5 still selected, drag the fill handle to extend the formula for the remaining columns. Figure 9.4 shows the results.

Figure 9.4.
Applying the
AVERAGE
function.

	A	B	C	D	E
1		13	65	-60	6
2		1	200	-259	14
3		8	-9	5	7
4	SUM	22	256	-314	27
5	AVERAGE	7.333333	85.33333	-104.667	9

The INT Function

This function returns the integer value of the result of an argument. An integer is any positive or negative number with no fractional or decimal part. The following are examples of integer values:-

6
347,755
-567
0

An argument for an INT function may consist of a single cell reference, constant or formula. The following are examples of valid INT functions:

=INT(45.67)
=INT(B12)
=INT(B8/100+R1)
=INT(SUM(PROFIT,6000),R28/C12)
(where PROFIT is an established Range Name)

A row will be added to the worksheet that contains the integer values of the average row.

1   A6   **INTEGER**

2   B6   **INT(B5)**

3   Use the fill handle to extend the formula to the remaining columns. Figure 9.5 shows the results.

Figure 9.5. Applying the INT function.

	A	B	C	D	E
1		13	65	-60	6
2		1	200	-259	14
3		8	-9	5	7
4	SUM	22	256	-314	27
5	AVERAGE	7.333333	85.33333	-104.667	9
6	INTEGER	7	85	-105	9

Note that the INT function always truncates a value at the decimal point. Thus when applied to a negative number as it is in cell D6, the number decreases in magnitude.

The ROUND Function

This function rounds values to a specified number of decimal places and takes the following format:-

=ROUND(value or cell reference or formula,no. of decimals)

The first part of the argument is the value to be rounded and the second specifies the number of decimal places required. This can be entered as a value, a cell reference, or be the result of a formula.

Valid examples of the ROUND function include:-

=ROUND(101.66678,2)
=ROUND(G20,0)
=ROUND(B4/C4,3)
=ROUND(D54,B5)
(where B5 contains a value representing the required number of decimal places)

The ROUND function differs from the formatting commands in that choosing to format cells only affects the way they are displayed, using the full level of accuracy for any calculation performed on the cell. The ROUND function, however, actually changes the value in the cell to the specified number of decimals and uses that value in any calculation.

Tip: *Format cells to the same number of decimal places as you round them, otherwise you may not have an accurate representation of the results.*

The following steps illustrate the different results that can be obtained through the use of ROUND, INT and formatting commands.

1   A9   **ROUND**

2   B9**101.678**

3   C9**=ROUND(B9,1)**

4   D9   **=INT(B9)**

5   E9 **101.678**

6   With cell E9 selected, click on the right mouse button and select *Format |
      Cell* and format the cell to two decimal places.

7   B10   **101.678**

8   C10   **=ROUND(B10,2)**

9   D10   **101.678**

10   With cell E10 selected, click on the right mouse button and select *Format
      | Cell* and format the cell to two decimal places.

11   Click on cell B11 and then on the *AutoSum* button to total the two rows
      above.

12   Use the fill handle to extend the formula to column E.

      Figure 9.6 shows the different results that can be returned depending on the
      way the values are manipulated.

*Figure 9.6.
Applying the
ROUND function.*

	A	B	C	D	E
1		13	65	-60	6
2		1	200	-259	14
3		8	-9	5	7
4	SUM	22	256	-314	27
5	AVERAGE	7.333333	85.33333	-104.667	9
6	INTEGER	7	85	-105	9
7					
8					
9	ROUND	101.678	101.7	101	101.68
10		101.678	101.68	101	101.68
11		203.356	203.38	202	203.356

Note: *You can round cells through the format command by selecting **Tools
| Options | Calculation** and check the Precision as Displayed box. The
problem with this approach is that you cannot easily see what you have done
to the cell, whereas the ROUND function is part of the formula and can be
seen on the edit line.*

The MAX Function

The MAX function is used to report the largest value in the specified arguments.

The MAX function will search a row, a column, a range or a combination of any of these. A constant or a formula may also be included in the MAX function. The following are valid examples of MAX.

> =MAX(4,6.5,100)
>
> =MAX(A1,B2,C3)
>
> =MAX(C3:E3,B2:B4,100)
>
> =MAX(0,A1/C2,E4*H6)

The last example above is particularly interesting. This formula has the effect of preventing a negative result being returned in the cell. Should the result of A1/C2 and E4*H6 be less than 0, the 0 becomes the maximum value. Such an expression is useful when calculating cells that must never return a negative result.

For example in a marketing plan that calculated that amount of money to be spent on advertising. One could argue that you cannot spend a negative amount on advertising and so instead of returning a negative result, zero could be returned as the result.

The MAX function will be used to report the maximum value in each column of the table.

1   A13   **MAXIMUM**

2   B13   **=MAX(B1:B11)**

3   Drag on the fill handle to extend the formula to column E. Figure 9.7 shows the effect of this function.

Figure 9.7.
Applying the MAX
function.

	A	B	C	D	E
1		13	65	-60	6
2		1	200	-259	14
3		8	-9	5	7
4	SUM	22	256	-314	27
5	AVERAGE	7.333333	85.33333	-104.667	9
6	INTEGER	7	85	-105	9
7					
8					
9	ROUND	101.678	101.7	101	101.68
10		101.678	101.68	101	101.68
11		203.356	203.38	202	203.356
12					
13	MAXIMUM	203.356	256	202	203.356

The MIN Function

The MIN function is the opposite to MAX in that it returns the smallest value in the range specified in the argument.

MIN searches a row, column, range or any combination of these. Constants and formulae may also be specified in the MIN function. Valid examples of MIN include:-

$$=MIN(6,3,6)$$
$$=MIN(B2:M2,B4:M4)$$
$$=MIN(PROFIT,1000,E5)$$
$$=MIN(I8:O12,C1:U1)$$
$$=MIN(F5/L7,AD4*AX40,10)$$

In the last example above, the effect of the formula is to prevent a result in excess of 10 being returned. If the result of F5/L7 or AD4*AX40 is greater than 10, the minimum value in the argument becomes 10.

The MIN function will be used to report the minimum value in each column of the table.

1   A14   **MINIMUM**

2   B14   **=MIN(B1:B11)**

3   Drag on the fill handle to extend the formula to column E. Figure 9.8 shows the effect of this function.

Figure 9.8.
Applying the MIN
function.

	A	B	C	D	E
1		13	65	-60	6
2		1	200	-259	14
3		8	-9	5	7
4	SUM	22	256	-314	27
5	AVERAGE	7.333333	85.33333	-104.667	9
6	INTEGER	7	85	-105	9
7					
8					
9	ROUND	101.678	101.7	101	101.68
10		101.678	101.68	101	101.68
11		203.356	203.38	202	203.356
12					
13	MAXIMUM	203.356	256	202	203.356
14	MINIMUM	1	-9	-314	6

The ABS Function

This function returns the magnitude or *absolute value* of its numeric argument. Thus a negative value becomes positive, and a positive value remains the same.

The argument for the ABS function may be a number or a formula. Valid examples of the function include:-

=ABS(4)
=ABS(-4)
=ABS(R4)
=ABS(R8/5-10)
=ABS(PROFIT)
(where PROFIT is an established range name)

In the following steps the absolute value of cells B14:E14 will be returned in row 15.

A15   **ABSOLUTE**

B15   **=ABS(B14)**

Drag the fill handle to extend the formula to column E. Figure 9.9 shows the results.

Figure 9.9.
Applying the ABS
function.

	A	B	C	D	E
1		13	65	-60	6
2		1	200	-259	14
3		8	-9	5	7
4	SUM	22	256	-314	27
5	AVERAGE	7.333333	85.33333	-104.667	9
6	INTEGER	7	85	-105	9
7					
8					
9	ROUND	101.678	101.7	101	101.68
10		101.678	101.68	101	101.68
11		203.356	203.38	202	203.356
12					
13	MAXIMUM	203.356	256	202	203.356
14	MINIMUM	1	-9	-314	6
15	ABSOLUTE	1	9	314	6

The COUNT Function

COUNT returns the number of value entries specified in the argument. The COUNT function will search individual cells, a row, column, range or any combination of these.

When calculating the result, the COUNT function ignores blank and text cells, but will count cells that contain values or formulae.

Valid examples of the COUNT function include:-

=COUNT(R1,C3:C5)

=COUNT(R10:V10)

=COUNT(ITEMS,A1):F20)

(where ITEMS is an established Range Name)

To see the effect of the COUNT function it will be applied to the range A1:E6.

A16   =COUNT(A1:E6)

The result is 24 as the blank cells and the text entries in column A are not counted.

Putting Functions to Practical Use

The functions that have been used in the table in Figure 9.8 are those which you will frequently require during model development, regardless of the application you are working on. To consolidate this section, some of the above functions can be used in conjunction with the TRENDY_N workbook in order to perform some additional analysis.

1   Open TRENDY_N.XLS

2   Save the file as TREN_FUN

The total of the Quarterly Totals column in cell F10 does not add up correctly on the screen because the cells have been formatted. To correct this the formulae in the range F5:F9 should include the ROUND function.

3   F5 =**ROUND(SUM(B5:E5),0)**

4   Drag the fill handle to extend the formula to cell F9. Figure 9.10 shows column F of the worksheet before and after applying the ROUND function.

Figure 9.10.
Before and after
applying the
ROUND function.

	F	G
4	Quarterly Total	Quarterly Total
5	(with round())	
6	28518	28518
7	27700	27700
8	30428	30428
9	22917	22917
10	22519	22519
11	132082	132081

A conservative estimate is preferred for the total monthly sales in row 10 and so the INT function can be applied in order to truncate, rather than round, the values.

5   B10   =**INT(SUM(B5:B9))**

6   Drag the fill handle to extend the formula to column E. Figure 9.11 shows the totals row before and after applying the INT function.

Figure 9.11.
Effect of applying
the INT function.

	A	B	C	D	E		F
10	Total Monthly Sales	£ 32,560	£ 32,865	£ 33,173	£ 33,484	£	132,081

	A	B	C	D	E		F
10	Total Monthly Sales	£ 32,560	£ 32,864	£ 33,172	£ 33,483	£	132,079

As a final addition to the file it would be useful to report the average sales for each month.

7   A12   **Average monthly sales**

8   B12   **=AVERAGE(B5:B9)**

9   Drag the fill handle to extend the formula to column E. Figure 9.12 shows the final worksheet with all the additional function in place.

Figure 9.12.
Worksheet
incorporating
additional
functions.

	A	B	C	D	E		F
1			TRENDY TOYS				
2			National Quarterly Sales Forecast				
3							
4		January	February	March	April		Quarterly Total
5	Baby & Toddler	7030	7096	7162	7230	£	28,518
6	Educational	6830	6893	6957	7021	£	27,700
7	Dolls	7500	7571	7642	7714	£	30,428
8	Models	5650	5703	5756	5809	£	22,917
9	Garden	5550	5603	5656	5710	£	22,519
10	Total Monthly Sales	£ 32,560	£ 32,864	£ 33,172	£ 33,483	£	132,079
11							
12	Average monthly sale	6512	6573	6635	6697		

Exercise

1	Open TRENDY_N and save it as TREN_FNX.
2	Calculate the average monthly sales for each location, rounded as displayed to two decimal places.
3	Report the maximum quarterly total for each location.

The Function Wizard

The Function Wizard can be used at any time you want to use a function. It helps you select the correct function and construct the arguments correctly as well as insert the function into your formula. The formula bar shows the changes you make as you build the formula.

The Function Wizard is activated by clicking on the *Function Wizard* button which displays the first of two dialogue boxes as shown in Figure 9.13.

Figure 9.13. Function Wizard step 1 dialogue box.

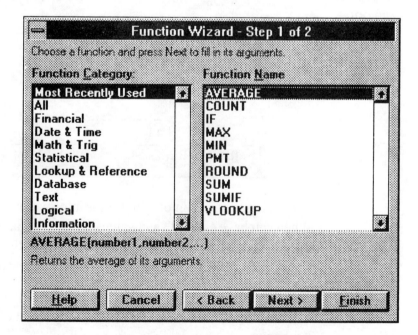

To the left is a list of the function categories and to the right is an alphabetical list of the functions in the selected category. In Figure 9.13 the 10 most recently used functions are being displayed.

When you click the *Finish* button the selected function is inserted into your formula with the argument names inserted as placeholders. For example, clicking *Finish* in Figure 9.13 inserts the following into the formula bar:-

You can then replace the argument text with the values necessary to complete the function.

If, instead of clicking the *Finish* button, you select *Next* from the Step 1 dialogue box, the Step 2 dialogue box will be displayed as shown in Figure 9.14.

Figure 9.14. Function Wizard step 2 dialogue box.

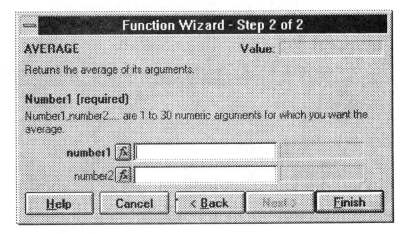

This dialogue box prompts you for the information that the function requires. When you have entered valid values for each argument, the calculated value for the function is displayed in the Value box at the top of the dialogue box. Clicking on *Finish* will insert the calculated value into your formula.

The function wizard is particularly useful when you are working with unfamiliar functions and if you have a complex set of arguments to insert into a function.

Incorporating Logic

Excel provides a series of functions that allows the system to logically analyse the contents of an active cell and take a course of action depending on whether the result of the condition is proved true or false. A logical function evaluated as true has a numeric value of 1, and one evaluated as false has a value of 0.

The IF Function

One of the most commonly used logical functions is IF which allows you to perform conditional tests on cells in the worksheet. IF takes the following form:-

IF(Proposition,*True*,*False*)

If the resultant check on the proposition evaluates as true, then the first option (*true*) will be taken. If it is false, the second option (*false*) is used.

For example:

=IF(J20=5,10,50)

which is interpreted as *if the contents of cell J20 are equal to 5, the result of this formula is 10, otherwise the result is 50.*

The logical operands that can be used in conjunction with a condition test are:-

=	equal to
>	greater than
<	less than
>=	greater than or equal to
<=	less than or equal to
<>	not equal to

The following examples illustrate various ways in which the IF function can be used and how the logic is interpreted.

=IF(J20>10,45,78)

If the contents of cell J20 is greater than 10, the result of the formula is 45, otherwise the result is 78.

To illustrate the use of a simple IF function a report will be added to the Totals sheet of the National Forecast for Trendy Toys in which the shortfalls for those categories with a sales forecast below the average will be reported.

1   Open the TRENDY_N file

2   Save it as TREN_LOG

3   A14   **Shortfall Report**

4   Copy the category labels from A5:A9 to A15:A19

5   B15   **=IF(B5<$B$12,$B$12-B5,"")**

This means that if cell B5 is less than the average in cell B12 you want to subtract the sales figure in B5 from the average and return this as the result. If the sales are greater than the average the cell should be left blank. The reference to B12 is absolute in order that the formula can be copied to the other categories and retain the reference to the average.

Note: *The use of two double quotes together means that the cell is to be left blank.*

Figure 9.15 shows the results of the above.

Using AND and OR

Multiple conditional checks can be made within the conditional test through the use of the AND and OR functions.

The OR function checks on up to 30 logical conditions and returns a true result if at least one condition is satisfied. AND on the other hand, again checks up to 30 logical conditions but only returns a true result if all conditions are satisfied.

*Figure 9.15.
Using an IF
function for
conditional
testing.*

	A	B	C	D	E
4		January	February	March	April
5	Baby & Toddler	7030	7096	7162	7230
6	Educational	6830	6893	6957	7021
7	Dolls	7500	7571	7642	7714
8	Models	5650	5703	5756	5809
9	Garden	5550	5603	5656	5710
10	**Total Monthly Sales**	32560	32864	33172	33483
11					
12	Average monthly sale	6512	6573	6635	6697
13					
14	**Shortfall Report**				
15	Baby & Toddler				
16	Educational				
17	Dolls				
18	Models	862	810	756	703
19	Garden	962	909	856	802

For example:

$$=IF(OR(A1=1,B1=2,C1=3),100,200)$$

If cell A1 is equal to 1, or if cell B1 is equal to 2 or if cell C1 is equal to 3, then the proposition is true and the result is 100, otherwise the result is 200.

$$=IF(OR(G10>15,(H10*1.5)>15),1,2)$$

If cell G10 is greater than 15, or if the result of cell H10 multiplied by 1.5 is greater than 15, then the proposition is true and the result is 1, otherwise the result is 2.

$$=IF(AND(A1=1,B1=2,C1=3),100,200)$$

If cell A1 is equal to 1, and cell B1 is equal to 2, and cell C1 is equal to 3, then the proposition is true and the result is 100, otherwise the result is 200.

Nesting IF Functions

Multiple IF functions can be incorporated into a single formula which means that when a proposition has been tested the true and/or false options can be further functions. For example:-

=IF(AND(B1*B2>100,C1*C2<1000),SUM(D1:D10),SUM(E1:E10))

If the result of multiplying cell B1 by B2 is greater than 100, and the result of multiplying cell C1 by C2 is less than 1000, then the proposition is true and the result is the sum of the values in the range D1 through D10, otherwise the result is the sum of the range E1 through E10.

=IF(A5=5,IF(J9=10,50,100),20)

If cell A5 is equal to 5 then look to see if cell J9 is equal to 10. If it is the result is 50. If A5 is equal to 5, but J9 is not equal to 10, then the result is 100 and if A5 is not equal to 5 the result is 20.

Working With Text

You can use string references in conjunction with logic functions which means that text can be entered as part of a condition, or as the result of a conditional test. The text must, however, be delimited with double quotes.

For example:

=IF(D10=0,"John","Jane")

If cell D10 equals zero then John will be returned as the result, otherwise Jane will be returned.

Text references can also be used as part of the proposition when testing data.

For example:

=IF(J8="NUTS","No change",K1/H1)

If cell J8 contains the word NUTS, then the result will be the words No change, otherwise the contents of cell K1 are divided by the contents of cell H1 and the result returned.

A further example of using text entries is to test the contents of a cell with a range name. In this case the range name is not enclosed in quotes as it is an actual cell reference. For example:-

=IF(PROFIT<=5%,"Poor",IF(PROFIT<=12.5%,"Fair",IF(PROFIT <=20%,"Good","Excellent")))

If the cell named PROFIT is less than or equal to 5% then return the word Poor. If PROFIT is more than 5% but less than or equal to 12.5% return the word Fair. If PROFIT is more than 12.5% but less than or equal to 20% return the word Good and if PROFIT is more than 20% return the word Excellent.

In the shortfall report on the TREN_FUN worksheet the IF function put a zero into those cells that had no shortfall. The formula can be changed so that *OK* is displayed instead.

1   B15   **=IF(B5<$B$12,$B$12-B5,"OK")**

2   Drag the fill handle to extend the formula across to cell E15 and then down to cell E19. Figure 9.16 shows the results.

Figure 9.16. Incorporating text into an IF function.

	A	B	C	D	E
14	Shortfall Report				
15	Baby & Toddler	OK	OK	OK	OK
16	Educational	OK	OK	OK	OK
17	Dolls	OK	OK	OK	OK
18	Models	862	810	756	703
19	Garden	962	909	856	802

Exercise

1   Open the TREN_FNX file

2   Add a column after the Total Quarterly Sales that displays *Poor*
        if sales are under £25,000, *Good* for sales in excess of £25,000
        and less than £30,000, and *Excellent* for sales in excess of
        £30,000.

LOOKUP Functions

The effect of the last example above is to perform a range check insomuch
as a different result is required depending on the profit level. As you can see
these formulae can become quite long, and it is often difficult to get the syntax
absolutely right, especially in terms of opening and closing parentheses. The
VLOOKUP and HLOOKUP functions provide a much clearer method of
working with ranges. These functions allow you to find an item of data that
is associated with another. In the above example you could look up the profit
percentage and return the message, *Poor*, *Good*, or *Fair*.

The format of the two functions are the same:-

=VLOOKUP([search value],[table range],[column offset])

=HLOOKUP([search value],[table range],[row offset])

The VLOOKUP function begins by comparing the search value with the first
column in the table range. It then returns an associated value in the same row,
offset by the specified number of columns.

For example, Figure 9.17 shows a section from a spreadsheet that reports the
percentage profit figures. Below that line a lookup table has been created in
order to produce an appropriate message depending on the profit figures.

Figure 9.17.
Example of a
VLOOKUP
function.

	A	B	C	D	E
1	Gross profit %	4%	10%	12.50%	30%
2					
3					
4	Lookup table				
5	0%	Poor			
6	5%	Fair			
7	12.50%	Good			
8	20%	Excellent			

The VLOOKUP function can now be used in cell B2 to find the correct reference to be displayed. The format of the formula is as follows:-

=VLOOKUP(B1,$A$5:$B$8,2)

This formula is interpreted as follows:-

Look for the contents of cell B1 in the first column of the table range A5:B8. When a match is found return the contents of the cell in the same row in the second column of the table range.

The function will look for an exact match in the first column of the table, but if it cannot find one it will use the next lowest value. Therefore in the case of the above formula the value 4% is not in the table, but the next lowest value is 0% and therefore *Poor* will be returned as the result. If 0% has not been included in the table the result would be ERR as the LOOKUP function would not be able to find a valid search value.

Note: *Values in the first column or row of a lookup table must be in ascending order when you are searching within ranges. If you have irregular numbers you must be searching for an exact match.*

The reference to the lookup table has been made absolute so that when the formula is copied to the remaining columns, the table reference remains fixed. Figure 9.18 shows the results.

Figure 9.18.
Results of a
lookup table.

	A	B	C	D	E
1	Gross profit %	4%	10%	12.50%	30%
2		Poor	Fair	Good	Excellent
3					
4	Lookup table				
5	0%	Poor			
6	5%	Fair			
7	12.50%	Good			
8	20%	Excellent			

The following example illustrates a simple lookup table to calculate the amount of bonus payable.

1   Create the worksheet shown in Figure 9.19 and save it as LOOKUP.

Figure 9.19.
Worksheet for
Lookup table.

	A	B	C	D	E
1		Q1	Q2	Q3	Q4
2	Sales	1000	2500	900	3000
3	Price	10	10.1	10.2	10.3
4	Revenue	10000	25250	9180	30900
5	Bonus				

The bonus is dependent on the revenue each period and has been specified as follows.

> If the revenue is less than £10,000 there is no bonus payable; if the revenue is between £10,000 and £15,000 there is a bonus of 1%; if the revenue is more than £15,000 and up to £20,000 there is a bonus of 2% and if the revenue is in excess of £20,000 the bonus payable is 3%.

2   The data required for the lookup table must be entered into the worksheet as shown in Figure 9.20.

3   **B5=VLOOKUP(B4,$A$8:$B$11,2)**

4   Drag on the fill handle to extend the range to cell E5.

5   Figure 9.21 shows the results.

Figure 9.20.
Lookup table for
bonuses.

	A	B	C	D	E
1		Q1	Q2	Q3	Q4
2	Sales	1000	2500	900	3000
3	Price	10	10.1	10.2	10.3
4	Revenue	10000	25250	9180	30900
5	Bonus				
6					
7					
8	0	0%			
9	10000	1%			
10	15000	2%			
11	20000	3%			

Figure 9.21.
Completed
bonus formula.

	A	B	C	D	E
1		Q1	Q2	Q3	Q4
2	Sales	1000	2500	900	3000
3	Price	10	10.1	10.2	10.3
4	Revenue	10000	25250	9180	30900
5	Bonus	10	75	0	90
6					
7					
8	0	0%			
9	10000	1%			
10	15000	2%			
11	20000	3%			

Note: *You could have oriented the lookup table the other way with the search values (revenue) across row 8 and the bonus percentages below in rwo 9 and then use the HLOOKUP function instead of VLOOKUP.*

You can have as many columns in a lookup table as you need so that you can return different information that is associated with the search values in the first column or row. For example in the above case you might have different bonus values for the third and fourth quarters which could be entered as a third column in the table and the formula in cell D5 would then be =B5*VLOOKUP(B5,$A$8:$B$11,3).

Tip: *Naming the table range makes referencing it easier as you only have to say, for example, $LTABLE instead of $A$8:$B$11.*

Exercise

> **1**   Open TRENDY_FX
>
> **2**   Using a lookup table produce a report that looks at the quarterly totals for each location and reports *OK* if sales are in excess of £20,000, *Good* if sales are in excess of £30,000 and *Excellent* if sales are in excess of £40,000.

Summary

This chapter has looked at only a few of the many functions available in Excel. However, if you can master the use of these by incorporating them into your plans you will increase the flexibility of your work and will be able to perform more analysis. Using the function wizard you will soon be looking for functions to help you perform tasks that you previously thought too difficult to attempt.

Self Test

1   What do you do if the range suggested by AutoSum is not what you require?

2   What must you be careful about when specifying a range to average?

3   What is the effect of the INT function and give an example of when it might be useful.

4   What is the difference between rounding a range to two decimal places with the ROUND function and using the Format command?

5   Give an example of when you might use the ABS function.

Given the worksheet below, how would you calculate the following: (Assume you are entering formulae in cells A10 through A14).

	A	B	C	D
1	1	8	15	4
2	-2	-4	0	-6
3	1000	500	700	900
4	95	180	360	290
5				
6	100			

6 If the highest value in row 1 is more than 15, multiply A6 by 10, otherwise multiply cell A6 by 5.

=IF(MIN(A1:D1>15),A6*10,A6*5)

7 If there is a positive value in row 2 return the message *"too high"*, otherwise report the total value of the row as an absolute value.

=IF(MAX(A2:D2)<0,"too high",SUM(ABS(A2:D2)))

8 If the sum of the values in row 3 is greater than 5,000 then return the average value of the range, otherwise return the total value.

=IF(SUM(A3:D3)>5000,avg(A3:D3),SUM(A3:D3))

9 Using IF functions, test each cell in row 4 and if the value is less than 100, multiply cell A6 by 1.01, if the value is between 101 and 200, multiply cell A6 by 1.05 and if the value is more than 200, multiply A6 by 1.10.

=IF(A4<=100,$A$6*1.01,IF(A4<=200,$A$6*1.05,$A$6*1.1))

10 Repeat question 9 using a LOOKUP function.

=$A$6*VLOOKUP(A4,$A$16:$B$18,2)

	A	B
15	Lookup Table	
16	0	1.01
17	100	1.05
18	200	1.1

TEN
List Management Techniques

Key Learning Points in the Chapter

- What is list management?
- Where lists can be stored
- Creating lists
- Sorting lists
- Filtering lists
- List management functions
- Working with external lists

Introduction

List management is the term used by Excel to refer to its ability to manage collections of information, or *databases* as they are formally known. Put simply, an Excel list or database is a collection of related information that is stored in an organised way. For example, it could represent details on all of the company's employees, or it could store information on each of the products or services that your organisation can provide.

These lists can be stored within an Excel workbook, in which case they are said to be *internal*, or they can be stored in separate files, in which case they are said to be *external*. External lists are stored in special formats that allow them to be easily accessed by applications such as Microsoft Access, Borland Paradox and Lotus Approach. These are known as *DataBase Management Systems* (DBMS) and in conjunction with Excel provide one of the most powerful ways to manage information.

Internal vs External Tables

Fortunately you need to have no knowledge of such applications to make use of internal lists. This feature provides many powerful and easy-to-use methods for handling information, all of which is stored in standard Excel worksheets and is edited and managed using standard Excel commands.

However, there are some disadvantage to using internal lists:

- The size of the list is limited to the size of a worksheet – 16,384 rows and 256 columns. You may think that you will never reach these limits, but it can be surprising to see just how quickly lists can grow.

- The entire list must be able to fit in memory, which again limits the amount of data you can manage.

- Data stored in internal lists tends to consume more disk space than data stored in external DBMS lists.

The solution in these cases is to store data as an external list, then use Excel to manage the data.

List Structure

However the information is stored, the list will have to obey some simple rules regarding its structure and layout. It is most likely that you will be working with internal lists, so that is what we will concentrate on. However, we will also introduce the use of external lists at the end of the chapter.

- Each lists needs to be stored in a worksheet. You can have more than one list on a worksheet, but a single list cannot span several worksheets.

- The list is arranged into rows and columns, referred to as *records* and *fields*. Each record stores information on a specific item in the list, such as a specific employee. Each field provides a particular piece of information about that item, such as the employees surname, their postcode or their salary. The overall layout is therefore rectangular, as each record must have the same number of fields.

- The first row in the list is special. It contains what are known as *field headings*. These are descriptive titles that are used to refer to the fields of information. They become important when you start to use the Excel features to manage the list. Each field heading must be unique within the list, and should meaningfully describe what each field represents.

These rules are illustrated graphically in Figure 10.1.

Figure 10.1.
List structure.

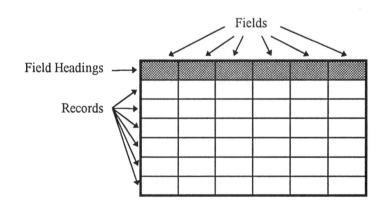

Whilst these three rules may seem quite stringent, in practice the creation of a list is very simple, and it is quite likely that you have already created lists that obey these rules many times before. Figure 10.2 shows a list that represents the products sold by Trendy Toys.

Figure 10.2.
Product list for
Trendy Toys.

	A	B	C	D	E	F	G
1	Product Listing for Trendy Toys						
2							
3	Code	Description	Cat	Unit Cost	Unit Price	Stock Qty	Avg Demand
4	1	Fluffy Bunny	B	2.50	4.75	86	24
5	2	Rag Doll	D	3.25	6.50	54	15
6	3	Football	G	1.75	3.95	116	38
7	4	Racing Car	M	4.50	7.25	57	21
8	5	Alphabet Shapes	E	2.75	3.95	63	17
9	6	Swing	G	12.50	17.50	17	4
10	7	Jet Plane	M	3.25	6.50	92	26
11	8	Cricket Set	G	6.75	9.25	37	13
12	9	Popup Pets	B	5.50	7.75	41	12
13	10	Building Blocks	E	4.75	6.75	25	23
14	11	Fighting Fred	D	4.25	8.25	72	31
15	12	Sailing Ship	M	5.25	8.50	43	19
16	13	Ninja Tortoise	D	3.25	7.75	124	41
17	14	Flying Scotsman	M	9.50	14.75	36	10
18	15	Quacking Duck	B	4.75	7.50	42	8
19	16	Talking Flower	E	3.50	6.25	18	6
20	17	Model T Ford	M	2.75	4.00	58	16
21	18	Paddling Pool	G	6.25	8.95	48	12
22	19	Weeping Wendy	D	4.50	9.75	24	10
23	20	Hopping Frog	B	1.75	3.75	62	22
24							

As you can see, the data is arranged into logical columns and rows, with each row (record) representing a separate product line, and each column (field) representing a particular attribute relating to the product. It is also clear that the field headings are in this case located in row 3 of the worksheet.

Establishing a Database

The creation of such a list is very straightforward. The exercises and examples throughout this chapter are based on the Trendy Toys product list, which should be created before proceeding:

1   Close all open workbooks, then create a new, blank workbook with the *New Workbook* button ☐.

2   In cell A1 of *Sheet 1*, enter the title of the sheet as **Product Listing for Trendy Toys**.

3   Enter the data for the list into the range A3:G23 according to the details shown in Figure 10.2 above. Remember to include field headings in row 3.

4   Highlight A3:G23 and select *Format | Column | AutoFit Selection* to set the column widths appropriately.

5   Save the workbook into the STEPXL directory as PROD_A.

In practice it is most likely that you will use data from other sources (such as existing spreadsheets or other applications) rather than creating a list from scratch. Therefore it is unlikely that you will actually have to type in a list of data as in this example, instead you will possibly be bringing information together from different locations, or positioning and formatting existing lists.

Sorting Lists

One of the most common requirements when working with lists of data is to sort them into order, depending on one or more fields. Excel makes this extremely quick and easy, providing both menu and button methods.

Sorting on a Single Field

To sort the list by a single field, you first select one of the cells in the field you want to sort by and then click one of the sort buttons. For example, to sort the product list according to the unit price field, with the most expensive items first (i.e. descending order):

1   Click the mouse in column E somewhere in the list; cell E5 for example.

2   Click on the *Sort Descending* button ⬚ on the Standard toolbar.

3   The list is sorted for you automatically, as shown in Figure 10.3.

Figure 10.3.
Product list sorted
by Unit Price,
descending.

Product Listing for Trendy Toys						
Code	Description	Cat	Unit Cost	Unit Price	Stock Qty	Avg Demand
6	Swing	G	12.50	17.50	17	4
14	Flying Scotsman	M	9.50	14.75	36	10
19	Weeping Wendy	D	4.50	9.75	24	10
8	Cricket Set	G	6.75	9.25	37	13
18	Paddling Pool	G	6.25	8.95	48	12
12	Sailing Ship	M	5.25	8.50	43	19
11	Fighting Fred	D	4.25	8.25	72	31
9	Popup Pets	B	5.50	7.75	41	12
13	Ninja Tortoise	D	3.25	7.75	124	41
15	Quacking Duck	B	4.75	7.50	42	8
4	Racing Car	M	4.50	7.25	57	21
10	Building Blocks	E	4.75	6.75	25	23
2	Rag Doll	D	3.25	6.50	54	15
7	Jet Plane	M	3.25	6.50	92	26
16	Talking Flower	E	3.50	6.25	18	6
1	Fluffy Bunny	B	2.50	4.75	86	24
17	Model T Ford	M	2.75	4.00	58	16
3	Football	G	1.75	3.95	116	38
5	Alphabet Shapes	E	2.75	3.95	63	17
20	Hopping Frog	B	1.75	3.75	62	22

Alternatively, to sort the list into ascending order on the product category, the following would be required:

1 Click the mouse in column C within the list; cell C20 for example.

2 Click on the *Sort Ascending* button $\boxed{\frac{A}{Z}\downarrow}$ on the Standard toolbar.

3 The list is now sorted according to the category, as shown in Figure 10.4.

4 Notice that within each category the records are still in descending order of unit price.

Figure 10.4.
Product list sorted
by Category,
ascending.

Product Listing for Trendy Toys						
Code	Description	Cat	Unit Cost	Unit Price	Stock Qty	Avg Demand
9	Popup Pets	B	5.50	7.75	41	12
15	Quacking Duck	B	4.75	7.50	42	8
1	Fluffy Bunny	B	2.50	4.75	86	24
20	Hopping Frog	B	1.75	3.75	62	22
19	Weeping Wendy	D	4.50	9.75	24	10
11	Fighting Fred	D	4.25	8.25	72	31
13	Ninja Tortoise	D	3.25	7.75	124	41
2	Rag Doll	D	3.25	6.50	54	15
10	Building Blocks	E	4.75	6.75	25	23
16	Talking Flower	E	3.50	6.25	18	6
5	Alphabet Shapes	E	2.75	3.95	63	17
6	Swing	G	12.50	17.50	17	4
8	Cricket Set	G	6.75	9.25	37	13
18	Paddling Pool	G	6.25	8.95	48	12
3	Football	G	1.75	3.95	116	38
14	Flying Scotsman	M	9.50	14.75	36	10
12	Sailing Ship	M	5.25	8.50	43	19
4	Racing Car	M	4.50	7.25	57	21
7	Jet Plane	M	3.25	6.50	92	26
17	Model T Ford	M	2.75	4.00	58	16

Note: *Having sorted the data in the list, the information in the worksheet is permanently reorganised into the new order. If you wanted to get back to the original order, you could use the Undo feature but this may have additional unwanted effects. A better approach is to add a unique record number field when the database is created, such as column A of the product listing. This field can be used to get the records back into their original positions by specifying it as the sort field.*

Returning the List to its Original Order

1   Click the mouse in column A within the list.

2   Click on the *Sort Ascending* button [A↓] on the Standard toolbar.

3   The list is returned to its original order.

Sorting on Multiple Fields

The above approach shows how a list can be sorted on multiple fields by performing several separate sorts, one on each field. This is not a very efficient way of achieving the objective though; a much better way is to specify all of the fields for sorting in one go.

For example, to sort the list by the product category, then within each category by average demand in descending order the following is required:

1 Click the mouse somewhere in the list. Whilst it is not strictly necessary, it is best to click in the column that you want to sort by so choose a cell in column C; C8 for example.

2 Select *Data | Sort*, and the dialogue box shown in Figure 10.5 is produced.

Figure 10.5. Sort dialogue box.

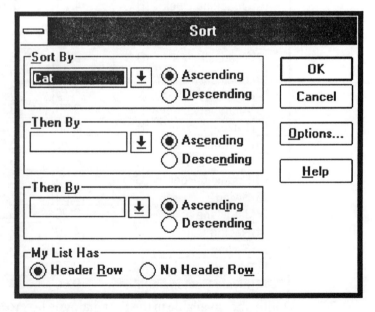

3 Since you clicked in column C, Excel suggests the field heading for this column as the first sort field. As this is correct you need not change any details here. If the incorrect heading is suggested select Cat from the list.

4   The second field for sorting is to be the average demand, so click the
        arrow in the *Then By* box to see the available field names. Scroll down the
        list and select *Avg Demand*. You could also have typed in a cell address
        for the column to be sorted, such as G5.

5   Click on the *Descending* button to set the sort order for this field.

6   Click *OK* to have Excel sort the list according to your specifications. The
        sorted list appears as shown in Figure 10.6.

Figure 10.6.
List sorted by
Category and
Average
Demand.

Product Listing for Trendy Toys						
Code	Description	Cat	Unit Cost	Unit Price	Stock Qty	Avg Demand
1	Fluffy Bunny	B	2.50	4.75	86	24
20	Hopping Frog	B	1.75	3.75	62	22
9	Popup Pets	B	5.50	7.75	41	12
15	Quacking Duck	B	4.75	7.50	42	8
13	Ninja Tortoise	D	3.25	7.75	124	41
11	Fighting Fred	D	4.25	8.25	72	31
2	Rag Doll	D	3.25	6.50	54	15
19	Weeping Wendy	D	4.50	9.75	24	10
10	Building Blocks	E	4.75	6.75	25	23
5	Alphabet Shapes	E	2.75	3.95	63	17
16	Talking Flower	E	3.50	6.25	18	6
3	Football	G	1.75	3.95	116	38
8	Cricket Set	G	6.75	9.25	37	13
18	Paddling Pool	G	6.25	8.95	48	12
6	Swing	G	12.50	17.50	17	4
7	Jet Plane	M	3.25	6.50	92	26
4	Racing Car	M	4.50	7.25	57	21
12	Sailing Ship	M	5.25	8.50	43	19
17	Model T Ford	M	2.75	4.00	58	16
14	Flying Scotsman	M	9.50	14.75	36	10

Options are available in the Sort dialogue box to specify whether your list has
a header row, and also through the *Options* button, whether your list is case
sensitive, ordered by rows or columns, and whether the first sort field (the
primary key) contains dates etc. In most cases, Excel correctly sets these
options for you so you are unlikely to need to change them.

Exercise

1	Return the product list to its original order.
2	Sort the list into descending order of stock quantity.
3	Sort the list into ascending order of average demand and unit cost.
4	Try to sort the list according to the amount of profit made on each product. **Hint**: *You need to add another field to the list.*

Filtering Lists

Whilst sorting a list gives you the ability to see the information in an orderly manner, it is not particularly helpful if there is a large amount of data. In this situation you may need to find a particular record (or multiple records) that meet certain conditions. This process is referred to as *filtering* the list, and allows you to quickly and easily locate the information that you want.

Excel provides two methods for filtering lists.

- *AutoFilter* allows you to display only those records in the list that meet specific *criteria*. The records are not duplicated, deleted or modified in any way by the AutoFilter process.

- *Advanced Filter* provides more control, for example, allowing you to copy the filtered records to a new location or to select only unique records. This is a more powerful facility but requires careful planning.

Using AutoFilter

AutoFilter can be switched on or off as desired:

1   Click the mouse in the list, for example on cell F10.

2   Select *Data | Filter | AutoFilter*.

3   Excel adds an arrow beside each field heading. If clicked, this produces a drop down list of the entries in that field.

Due to the width of the arrow, you may want to widen the columns again to ensure that the full field heading can be seen. Figure 10.7 shows the list after these changes have been made.

Figure 10.7.
Using AutoFilter.

	A	B	C	D	E	F	G
1	Product Listing for Trendy Toys						
2							
3	Code ⬇	Description ⬇	Cat ⬇	Unit Cost ⬇	Unit Price ⬇	Stock Qty ⬇	Avg Demand ⬇
4	1	Fluffy Bunny	B	2.50	4.75	86	24
5	2	Rag Doll	D	3.25	6.50	54	15
6	3	Football	G	1.75	3.95	116	38
7	4	Racing Car	M	4.50	7.25	57	21
8	5	Alphabet Shapes	E	2.75	3.95	63	17
9	6	Swing	G	12.50	17.50	17	4
10	7	Jet Plane	M	3.25	6.50	92	26
11	8	Cricket Set	G	6.75	9.25	37	13
12	9	Popup Pets	B	5.50	7.75	41	12
13	10	Building Blocks	E	4.75	6.75	25	23
14	11	Fighting Fred	D	4.25	8.25	72	31
15	12	Sailing Ship	M	5.25	8.50	43	19
16	13	Ninja Tortoise	D	3.25	7.75	124	41
17	14	Flying Scotsman	M	9.50	14.75	36	10
18	15	Quacking Duck	B	4.75	7.50	42	8
19	16	Talking Flower	E	3.50	6.25	18	6
20	17	Model T Ford	M	2.75	4.00	58	16
21	18	Paddling Pool	G	6.25	8.95	48	12
22	19	Weeping Wendy	D	4.50	9.75	24	10
23	20	Hopping Frog	B	1.75	3.75	62	22
24							
25							

Having enabled AutoFilter it can be used to display selected records only. For example, if you wanted to display only products in category M:

1   Click on the arrow next to the *Cat* field heading in column C. Figure 10.8 shows the list produced.

Figure 10.8.
AutoFilter list for
the Category
field.

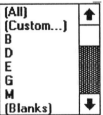

2   Click on the *M* category entry in the list.

3   Only those records with a category of M are displayed, as shown in Figure 10.9.

Figure 10.9. Filtering the list to show only Models.

	A	B	C	D	E	F	G
1	Product Listing for Trendy Toys						
2							
3	Code ⬇	Description ⬇	Cat ⬇	Unit Cost ⬇	Unit Price ⬇	Stock Qty ⬇	Avg Demand ⬇
7	4	Racing Car	M	4.50	7.25	57	21
10	7	Jet Plane	M	3.25	6.50	92	26
15	12	Sailing Ship	M	5.25	8.50	43	19
17	14	Flying Scotsman	M	9.50	14.75	36	10
20	17	Model T Ford	M	2.75	4.00	58	16
24							

When you are filtering lists in this way, Excel displays the either *Filter Mode* indicator, or the result of the last filter (such as *5 of 20 records found*) on the Status Bar.

Filtering with Ranges

You can of course use AutoFilter with multiple fields, by selecting the filter arrow for a different column and choosing one of the entries. However, it is perhaps more likely that instead of requiring a single match within a field you want to match a range of values. The *(Custom ...)* entry on the filter list can be used for this purpose.

For example, if you wanted to view all records that had an average demand of less than 10 units:

1   Click on the arrow to the right of the *Avg Demand* field heading in cell G3.

2   From the list that is displayed, choose the *(Custom...)* option. The dialogue box shown in Figure 10.10 is displayed.

Figure 10.10.
Custom AutoFilter
dialogue box.

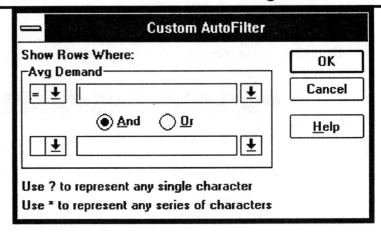

3   The details in this dialogue box define which records will be displayed. The first drop down box on the left shows the *comparison operator*, currently an "equals" sign (=). Click on the arrow to display the list, and select the "less than" sign (<).

4   Click in the box to the right of the comparison operator and type in the number you want to compare the records with, **10**.

5   Click on *OK* to apply this custom filter to the list, which will appear as shown in Figure 10.11.

Figure 10.11.
Filtering the list to
show records with
an average
demand of less
than 10.

	A	B	C	D	E	F	G
1	Product Listing for Trendy Toys						
2							
3	Code	Description	Cat	Unit Cost	Unit Price	Stock Qty	Avg Demand
9	6	Swing	G	12.50	17.50	17	4
18	15	Quacking Duck	B	4.75	7.50	42	8
19	16	Talking Flower	E	3.50	6.25	18	6
24							
25							

The custom filter provides great flexibility, as it can be used to create precise sets of conditions for viewing records. Each field can have its own custom AutoFilter settings, each consisting of one or two comparisons.

The different comparison operators behave the same way as if they had been used in a worksheet formula:

=	Values must match the criteria.	

=   Values must match the criteria.

>   Values must be greater than the criteria.

<   Values must be less than the criteria.

>=   Values must be greater than, or equal to, the criteria.

<=   Values must be less than, or equal to, the criteria.

< >   Values must be not equal to the criteria.

Wildcards can be used to form partial matches, with a "**?**" character being used to match a single character, and a "*****" being used to match any number of characters. For example, to find the products that begin with P you can enter P* and if you wanted the products beginning with PU you could enter PU*. If you looking for items with codes of six character, the first two changing and the last four 1Z1S, you could enter ??1Z1S.

Editing Filtered Records

Once you have successfully filtered the list to show only the records that you require, the details can be edited in the same way as normal cells. For example, having filtered the list to show only products with an average demand of less than 10 units:

1   Click on cell G18, the *Avg Demand* field for the *Quacking Duck*. Whilst this has a row number of 18, due to the filtering it will appear to be only the fifth row on screen.

2   Change the value from **8** to **18**.

3   Note that the list is *not* automatically filtered after this change. If you wanted to reapply the filter you would need to click on the *(Custom ...)* option in the AutoFilter menu in cell G3.

Displaying All Records

Once you have finished filtering the records you can redisplay all information in several different ways:

- The easiest is to turn off AutoFilter by selecting *Data | Filter | AutoFilter* to remove the checkmark from the menu option.

- If you just wanted to display everything, but leave AutoFilter enabled, then select *Data | Filter | Show All*, which has the same effect as activating each AutoFilter list in the field headings and choosing the *(All)* option for every one.

Once you display all the records using either of these techniques, the Status Bar indicator changes back to *Ready*, rather than showing *Filter Mode* or the results of the most recent filter.

To ensure that you can complete the following exercises correctly, select the *Data | Filter | Show All* command to display all records in the list.

Exercise

---

1   Use AutoFilter to show only those products whose names begin with an "F". **Hint**: The wildcard characters can be used for this.

2   Use AutoFilter to show only those records in the list that have a unit price of £8.50 or more. Remember to remove the original filter before applying this one to correctly display the matching records.

3   Use AutoFilter to show only products with a stock quantity of between 50 and 100 units. **Hint:** *You will need to use both comparisons in the Custom AutoFilter dialogue box.*

Advanced Filtering

In addition to AutoFilter, Excel offers a more flexible filtering technique through the *Data | Filter | Advanced Filter* command. When selected, this produced the dialogue box shown in Figure 10.12.

Options within this dialogue box allow you more control over the filtering process.

*Figure 10.12.
Advanced Filter
dialogue box.*

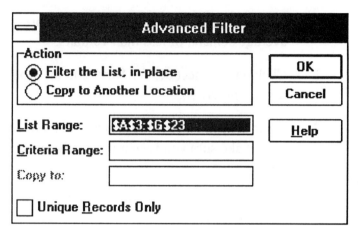

- The first selection, *Action*, allows you to choose whether the list will be filtered in place (similar to AutoFilter) or whether the matching records will be copied to a new area of the spreadsheet. This latter technique is often known as *extracting*, and is useful if you want to modify or change some of the details in the records but you don't want to update the original information.

- The *List Range* specifies the cell addresses of the list. This is correctly identified by Excel in the majority of cases.

- The *Criteria Range* specifies a separate area of the spreadsheet that is used to define the filtering criteria, rather than selecting them from lists as was the case with AutoFilter.

- The *Copy To* location is used only if you have chosen to extract the filtered records to another location.

- The *Unique Records Only* checkbox allows you to specify that duplicates will be ignored, so only one copy of each matching record will be displayed after filtering.

Defining Criteria

One of the first stages of using the advanced filter is to define the criteria for the matching records. As mentioned above, these are entered into a special range of the spreadsheet (the *criteria range*) rather than selecting them from lists.

For example, if you want to filter all records in the product list that have an average demand of less than 10 units:

1   Click on the sheet tab for *Sheet 2* in the workbook. We will use this sheet for storing criteria.

2   Enter the heading for the criteria field into cell A3 as **Avg Demand**. You must make sure you type it in exactly the same way as it was entered in the main list.

   In practice you may find it easier to copy these headings rather than retyping them every time.

3   Enter the criteria for filtering into cell A4: **<10**.

Filtering the List

Having defined the criteria you can use it to filter the list:

1   Click on the *Sheet 1* sheet tab, then click anywhere in the list; cell B6 for example.

2   Select *Data | Filter | Advanced Filter*.

3   Click in the *Criteria Range* box.

4   Click on the sheet tab for *Sheet 2*.

5   Click and drag over cells A3:A4 to highlight your criteria, including the field heading.

6   Click on the *OK* button to apply the filter to the list.

   Once filtered, the list appears as shown in Figure 10.13.

Figure 10.13.
The filtered list.

	A	B	C	D	E	F	G
1	Product Listing for Trendy Toys						
2							
3	Code	Description	Cat	Unit Cost	Unit Price	Stock Qty	Avg Demand
9	6	Swing	G	12.50	17.50	17	4
18	15	Quacking Duck	B	4.75	7.50	42	8
19	16	Talking Flower	E	3.50	6.25	18	6
24							
25							

As you would expect, exactly the same records are displayed as were produced using the AutoFilter approach, and therefore you may wonder why advanced filtering is necessary. In fact its true power becomes clearer when you want to use multiple criteria.

Multiple Criteria

It is awkward to use AutoFilter to filter records that match a criteria for one field or a criteria for another. Advanced filter makes this much easier. For example, if we wanted to filter those records in the product list that had an average demand of more than 30 units, or a stock quantity of more than 90 units:

1   Click in the product list and select *Data | Filter | Show All* to display all the records once more.

2   Activate *Sheet 2* by clicking its sheet tab, and change the criteria in cell A4 to >**30**.

3   Add a heading in cell B3 for the second criteria field: **Stock Qty**. Again this must be entered exactly as it appears in the main list.

4   Add the criteria for the stock quantity in cell B5: >**90**. Note that this is on the row beneath the criteria for the average demand. If they were on the same row then both criteria would have to be satisfied for the record to be displayed.

5   Activate *Sheet 1* again, and click in the list.

6   Select *Data | Filter | Advanced Filter*, and specify the *Criteria Range* as cells A3:B5 on *Sheet 2*, then click the *OK* button.

The filtered list appears as shown in Figure 10.14.

Figure 10.14.
List filtered using
multiple criteria.

	A	B	C	D	E	F	G
1	Product Listing for Trendy Toys						
2							
3	Code	Description	Cat	Unit Cost	Unit Price	Stock Qty	Avg Demand
6	3	Football	G	1.75	3.95	116	38
10	7	Jet Plane	M	3.25	6.50	92	26
14	11	Fighting Fred	D	4.25	8.25	72	31
16	13	Ninja Tortoise	D	3.25	7.75	124	41
24							
25							

Computed Criteria

Perhaps one of the most powerful features of advanced filtering is its ability to use computed criteria, in other words the result of a formula. For example, if you wanted to find all products for which there was not sufficient stock to satisfy demand for the next three months:

1   Activate *Sheet 2* by clicking its sheet tab.

2   In cell D3 enter a heading for this criteria: **Sufficient Stock**. Note that this should *not* be the same as an existing field heading.

3   In cell D4 enter the criteria: **=F4<G4*3**. Each time you use a computed criteria such as this you will do so by specifying the cell address of the field for the first record in the list. Note that there is no need to specify a sheet identifier as the criteria will be assumed to be relevant to the sheet containing the list.

4   Once entered, this cell shows a value of *FALSE*, as the first record in the list does not match the criteria. The filtering process will apply the criteria to each record in turn in a similar way.

5   Activate *Sheet 1* again and click anywhere on the list.

6   Select *Data | Filter | Advanced Filter.*

7   Set the criteria range to be cells D3:D4 on *Sheet 2*.

8   Click *OK* to have the list filtered on your computed criteria.

The filtered list appears as shown in Figure 10.15.

Figure 10.15.
Filtering a list with
computed criteria.

	A	B	C	D	E	F	G
				PROD_A.XLS			
1	Product Listing for Trendy Toys						
2							
3	Code	Description	Cat	Unit Cost	Unit Price	Stock Qty	Avg Demand
7	4	Racing Car	M	4.50	7.25	57	21
11	8	Cricket Set	G	6.75	9.25	37	13
13	10	Building Blocks	E	4.75	6.75	25	23
14	11	Fighting Fred	D	4.25	8.25	72	31
15	12	Sailing Ship	M	5.25	8.50	43	19
22	19	Weeping Wendy	D	4.50	9.75	24	10
23	20	Hopping Frog	B	1.75	3.75	62	22
24							

Working with Filtered Lists

Having filtered a list using either AutoFilter or Advanced Filter, many of the standard Excel commands, buttons and features work only on the filtered records. For example, if you filter a list then highlight a number of records and press the DEL key, only the displayed records are deleted; any hidden information remains unaffected.

The same applies when sorting, formatting, charting or even using the AutoSum feature for totalling. Furthermore some features such as charting and using AutoSum are dynamic – if you later change the filter to display a different selection of records, the chart or AutoSum total changes to reflect the new matches.

Exercise

1   Use *Advanced Filter* to display only those records with a Unit Cost of less than £4.00 OR a Unit Price of less than £6.00.

2   Use *Advanced Filter* to display only those records with a Unit Cost of less than £4.00 AND a Unit Price of less than £6.00.

Exercise cont.

---

3   Use *Advanced Filter* to display only those records for products that make a profit of more than £4.00. **Hint:** *you can compute the profit as the difference between Unit Price and Unit Cost.*

List Management Functions

In addition to filtering records to obtain details, it is also possible to use *database functions* to obtain information for specific records or groups of records.

Database functions require three items of information, or *arguments*:

- The first is the range that contains the list, including the field headings. Using the product list this would be the range A3:G23.

- The second is the heading of the field that is to be computed.

- The third is the range that contains the criteria, again including the field headings. This is similar in structure to the Advanced Filter criteria range.

For example, if you wanted to count the number of products in category M:

1   Activate Sheet 1 in PROD_A.XLS.

2   Enter the heading for the criteria field into cell B30: **Cat**

3   Enter the value to be matched into cell B31: **M**

4   Enter a heading for the result into cell F30: **Record Count**.

5   Enter the database function into cell F31:
=DCOUNTA(A3:G23,"Cat",B30:B31)

6   Excel counts the number of entries in the list with a category of "M", correctly returning the number 5.

Note that it was necessary to use the DCOUNTA function in this example, as the field that was summarised (Cat) contained text. If we had counted the entries in a numeric field (such as Code) then the DCOUNT function could have been used instead.

Just as with advanced filtering, the criteria range for a database function can have several fields or several entries for a single field. For example, if you wanted to total the stock quantity for all products in category M that have a unit price of £7.50 or greater:

1 Enter the heading for the second criteria field into cell C30: **Unit Price**

2 Enter the comparison for the second criteria into cell C31: >=7.5

3 Enter a heading for the total in cell G30: **Total Stock**.

4 Enter the database function into cell G31:
=DSUM(A3:G23,"Stock Qty",B30:C31)

5 Excel performs the calculation and returns the result 79.

Other database functions cater for different calculations, including DAVERAGE, DGET, DMAX, DMIN, DPRODUCT, DSTDEV and DVAR. These are fully documented in the Excel reference manuals, and can be found in the help system by searching for them by name, or under the heading of "Worksheet Functions".

Changing Criteria

Because database functions are dynamic, any changes to the criteria cause the result of the function to be re-evaluated in the same way as any normal worksheet formula. Therefore you can easily investigate the effects of different set of criteria values.

For example, to total the stock quantity for all products in category M that have a unit price of £5.00 or greater:

1 Click in cell C31 and change the criteria to >=5.

2   Excel immediately recalculates the total in cell G31, displaying the new result as 228.

SUMIF and COUNTIF

Two list management functions that are required more often than most are summation and counting. Therefore specific functions have been provided to make these calculations easier and quicker: SUMIF and COUNTIF.

SUMIF takes three criteria:

- The first is the range of cells that will be examined.

- The second is the criteria (in text format) that will be used for matching.

- The third is the range of cells that are to be totalled.

For example, if you wanted to calculate the total stock held of all products in category G, the following function would be required:

=SUMIF(C4:C23, ,"G",F4:F23)

COUNTIF takes only two criteria:

- The first is the range of cells that will be examined.

- The second is the criteria that will be used.

For example, to count the number of products that have an average demand of more than 25 units the following would be required:

=COUNTIF(G4:G23,">25")

Both of these functions can be used not only with formal lists, but any collection of data that occupies a contiguous range of cells.

Exercise

1   Calculate the average stock quantity for all products in category D.

Exercise cont.

> **2** Determine the number of items that have a unit price of less than £5.00.

Working with External Lists

In addition to working with internal lists, Excel can access data that is stored in a DBMS format. This feature is provided through the Microsoft Query product, which is supplied with Excel as an add-in option that needs to be selected during installation. You can see if you have already installed Microsoft Query by looking at the bottom of the *Data* menu. If the last option is *Get External Data* then query is available, otherwise you need to rerun the Setup utility.

Once installed, selecting *Data* | *Get External Data* causes the XLQUERY.XLA add-in to be loaded from disk, which in turn executes the Microsoft Query application. Query is then used to select a database, filter records, sort records, and then to return the values to Excel. Once the information has been transferred to Excel the data can be manipulated as if it were an internal list.

However the crucial difference is that Query is able to work with much larger databases than is possible within Excel alone, and is therefore an ideal way of obtaining information from corporate data sources such as accounting systems or client databases.

The use of MS Query is beyond the scope of this textbook, but the application and its interaction is documented in the Excel manuals, in the help system, and in many other textbooks as well, primarily those aimed at users already experienced with Excel 5.

Other List Management Features

Excel has several other features that make it easier to manage and analyse lists of data. For example, selecting *Data | Subtotals* allows you to specify that subtotals should be added to your list. You can choose which fields you want to summarise, and how you want the subtotals to be derived. For example,

Figure 10.16 shows subtotals added to the product list after it has been sorted by category.

Figure 10.16. Subtotals added to the list.

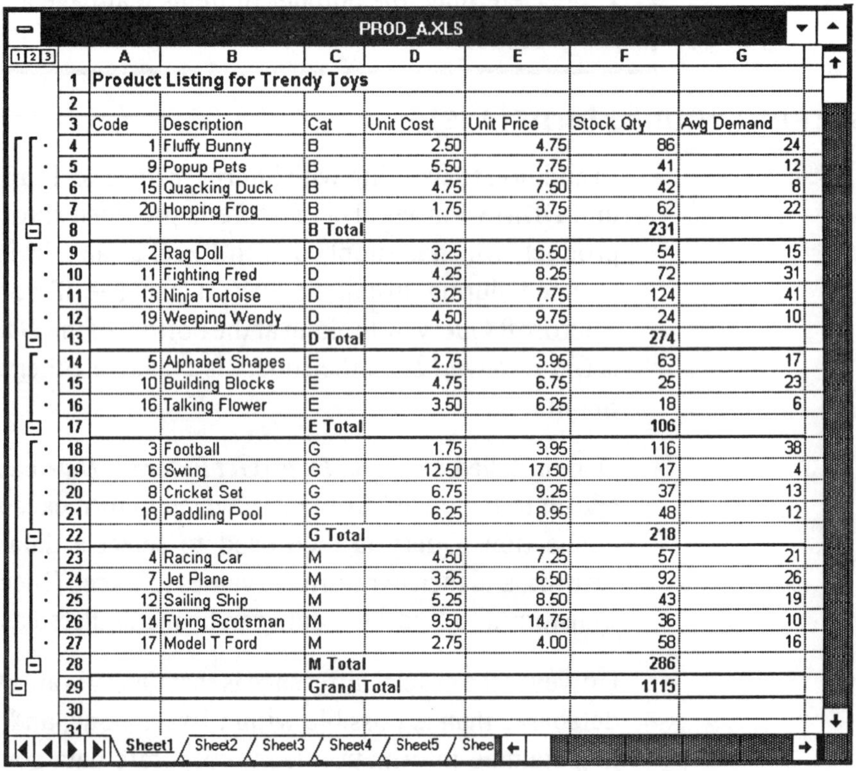

PROD_A.XLS

	A	B	C	D	E	F	G
1	Product Listing for Trendy Toys						
2							
3	Code	Description	Cat	Unit Cost	Unit Price	Stock Qty	Avg Demand
4	1	Fluffy Bunny	B	2.50	4.75	86	24
5	9	Popup Pets	B	5.50	7.75	41	12
6	15	Quacking Duck	B	4.75	7.50	42	8
7	20	Hopping Frog	B	1.75	3.75	62	22
8			B Total			231	
9	2	Rag Doll	D	3.25	6.50	54	15
10	11	Fighting Fred	D	4.25	8.25	72	31
11	13	Ninja Tortoise	D	3.25	7.75	124	41
12	19	Weeping Wendy	D	4.50	9.75	24	10
13			D Total			274	
14	5	Alphabet Shapes	E	2.75	3.95	63	17
15	10	Building Blocks	E	4.75	6.75	25	23
16	16	Talking Flower	E	3.50	6.25	18	6
17			E Total			106	
18	3	Football	G	1.75	3.95	116	38
19	6	Swing	G	12.50	17.50	17	4
20	8	Cricket Set	G	6.75	9.25	37	13
21	18	Paddling Pool	G	6.25	8.95	48	12
22			G Total			218	
23	4	Racing Car	M	4.50	7.25	57	21
24	7	Jet Plane	M	3.25	6.50	92	26
25	12	Sailing Ship	M	5.25	8.50	43	19
26	14	Flying Scotsman	M	9.50	14.75	36	10
27	17	Model T Ford	M	2.75	4.00	58	16
28			M Total			286	
29			Grand Total			1115	
30							
31							

Sheet1 / Sheet2 / Sheet3 / Sheet4 / Sheet5 / Shee

The symbols to the left of the row identifiers are outline symbols, and allow the list to be collapsed to show subtotals or grand totals only. For example, Figure 10.17 shows the list collapsed by one level.

Figure 10.17. Subtotals only display.

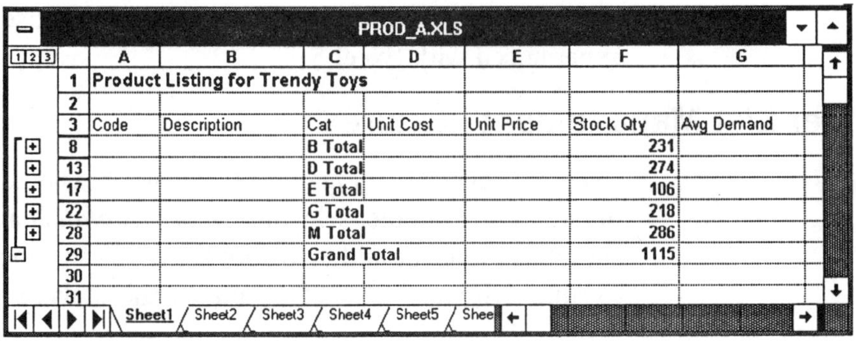

PROD_A.XLS

	A	B	C	D	E	F	G
1	Product Listing for Trendy Toys						
2							
3	Code	Description	Cat	Unit Cost	Unit Price	Stock Qty	Avg Demand
8			B Total			231	
13			D Total			274	
17			E Total			106	
22			G Total			218	
28			M Total			286	
29			Grand Total			1115	
30							
31							

Sheet1 / Sheet2 / Sheet3 / Sheet4 / Sheet5 / Shee

Another way of having Excel analyse the data for you is through the use of a Pivot Table. This is a special tabular layout than can be applied to any list of data, either internal or external.

The **Data | PivotTable** command is used to activate the Pivot Table Wizard, which takes you step by step through the creation of the table.

- The first step requires that you specify the source of the data to be summarised. For example it could be an internal list.

- The second step involves the definition of the exact location, such as the range of cells that contain the internal list.

- The third step involves the design of the table itself, using a drag-and-drop approach to specify what information should be shown in columns, rows, and the summarised area of the table.

- The fourth step allows you to choose the location of the Pivot Table within your workbook, as well as adding totals, titles etc.

Figure 10.18 shows a very simple Pivot Table created from the product list to show the different stock quantities held for each category.

Figure 10.18. A simple Pivot Table.

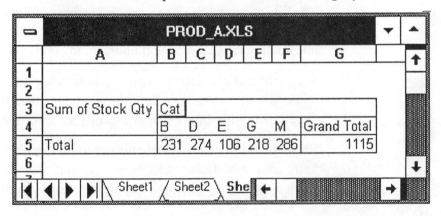

Figure 10.19 shows a more sophisticated Pivot Table that summarises the sales by country, region and sales person. In tabular form this information is quite easy to understand; in its original list form it was almost meaningless.

Figure 10.19. Pivot Table summarising sales by employee and region.

		EMPLOYEE									
Country	Region	J Smith	E Edwards	K Armitage	F Windsor	B Lawrence	T Higgs	R Peters	N Brown	S Collins	Grand Total
Canada	BC	0	0	0	0	0	0	0	1316.95	0	1316.95
Canada Total		0	0	0	0	0	0	0	1316.95	0	1316.95
UK	Kent	0	0	0	0	0	589.05	0	0	0	589.05
	Suffolk	0	0	0	747	0	0	0	0	0	747
	(blank)	841.5	0	0	1148	1423.5	0	3345.9	3205.5	0	9964.4
UK Total		841.5	0	0	1895	1423.5	589.05	3345.9	3205.5	0	11300.45
USA	AK	863.96	0	0	0	0	0	0	0	0	863.96
	AZ	0	0	1171	0	0	0	0	0	0	1171
	CA	0	0	560.4	192.1	0	0	0	0	351	1103.5
	CO	0	0	371	0	0	0	0	0	0	371
	ID	0	0	2052.68	0	0	0	0	0	0	2052.68
	MT	0	0	0	1405	17.4	0	0	968.18	0	2390.58
	NM	0	0	0	3485.35	0	0	0	0	0	3485.35
	NY	1984.83	0	97.3	0	173.4	0	0	0	0	2255.53
	OR	909.91	135	860.5	0	0	1057.6	0	0	0	2963.01
	TX	0	438.43	3194.2	0	0	0	0	0	0	3632.63
	WA	671.5	1418	731.8	0	0	0	91.8	182.08	0	3095.18
USA Total		4430.2	1991.43	9028.88	5082.45	190.8	1057.6	91.8	1150.26	351	23374.42
Grand Total		5271.7	1991.43	9028.88	6977.45	1614.3	1646.65	3437.7	5672.71	351	35991.82

One of the key features about the Pivot Table is that it is dynamic, so any changes to the original information can be immediately reflected in the Pivot Table. Furthermore, if you decide that a different layout for the table would have been better, you need only select *Data | PivotTable* again to access the design step of the Pivot Table wizard. Therefore subsequent modification is very quick and easy.

Summary

The lists and database management features of Excel are unrivalled by other spreadsheet applications, especially from the point of view of making the information easy to read and understand.

Simple operations such as sorting and filtering lists can be performed with a minimum of keystrokes or mouse clicks, thereby encouraging you to experiment with different analyses of your information.

Presentation of quantities of information is greatly eased by the provision of automatic subtotalling and outlining, and also through the use of Pivot Tables, especially when used in conjunction with external data sources.

Self Test

1 What is the maximum number of records that can be held in an internal list?

2 What is the maximum number of fields that can be stored in an internal list?

3 Are there any limits on the number of records and fields stored in external lists?

4 What special considerations are there when entering details from a personnel register into a worksheet so that the Excel list management features can be used?

5 Assuming you had a list of customers which included a field showing average monthly expenditure, what is the easiest way to sort the list so that those customers spending most were listed first?

6 Describe two ways of sorting a list on two separate fields, for example first by County and then by Postal Town?

7 How could you display those customers located in London?

8 How could you display those customers located in London or Edinburgh?

9 How could you display only those customers with an average monthly spend of £50,000 or greater?

10 How could you display the expected total monthly income from those customers located in London or Sheffield?

ELEVEN
Macros

Key Learning Points in this Chapter

- What is a spreadsheet macro?

- Creating macros

- Executing macros

- Assigning a toolbar button to the macro

Introduction

Macros are among the most powerful features of any application, and have been present in most PC applications since the early commercial software packages became available. Put simply, a macro is a sequence of commands or keystrokes that is stored within the program in a form that can quickly be recalled and executed. This means that they can be used to speed up repetitive tasks, to automate complex routines and to simplify the process of using the application.

Each macro language tends to use a completely different set of commands. Some, such as the early spreadsheets, are little more than sets of keystrokes, whilst the more modern software usually implements macros using English-like commands and statements. Excel 5 falls into the latter category, as it incorporates a development language called Visual Basic, which makes the macros relatively easy to read and understand. This obviously helps somewhat when it comes to working with macros, although as you will see, it is not strictly necessary to understand the commands in order to make use of them.

What are Macros Used For?

As noted previously, macros can be used for many different tasks including speeding up and automating repetitive procedures. Macros can also be used to automate an entire process, allowing you to write a complete spreadsheet management system.

For example, a macro-driven system could be written to ask the user which department's budget they wanted to work with or create, and then automatically load the appropriate file or create a fresh spreadsheet. It could then guide the user through the steps of data entry, verification, charting and printing, finally producing the output according to a predefined style.

Where are Macros Stored?

Excel stores macros in special macro sheets, either in a normal workbook or in a Personal Macro Workbook. When you create the macro you need to choose where it will be stored, as this will have a bearing on when it can be used.

Using a Standard Workbook

Macros stored in normal workbooks can only be used when that workbook is loaded into memory. Therefore this approach may not be suitable for macros that you will use on a day-to-day basis as you would have to load the workbook every time.

Using the Personal Macro Workbook

Macros stored in the Personal Macro Workbook are globally available, and can be called and accessed at any time. Therefore this approach is preferred for general purpose macros, such as those you might use to speed up tasks such as formatting, working with graphics, and printing.

However, if too many macros are stored in the Personal macro Workbook then you may become confused as to exactly which ones you should be working with at any time. As you will see, the use of descriptive macro names helps to solve this problem.

How are Macros Created?

Two approaches can be used for creating macros; recording or writing. These techniques are complimentary, with recorded macros often being used as the basis for a complete written macro.

Recording Macros

Recording a macro to automate something is as easy as going through that process manually. The only difference is that prior to starting the procedure you switch on the macro recorder. From that point on, every keystroke or command that you issue will be recorded by the system until you turn the macro recorder off again.

The main macro dialogue box is accessed by selecting the *Tools | Record Macro | Record New Macro* menu commands, which produces the box shown in Figure 10.1.

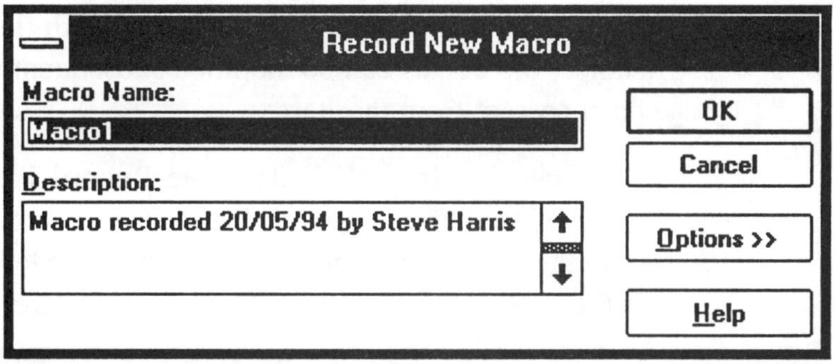

*Figure 10.1.
The Record New
Macro dialogue
box.*

This dialogue box provides the most common details that are required when recording a macro – the name and the description. If this is all that needs to be defined, clicking the *OK* button starts recording. However, if you want to define further attributes for the macro then the *Options* button can be clicked to produce the expanded dialogue box shown in Figure 10.2.

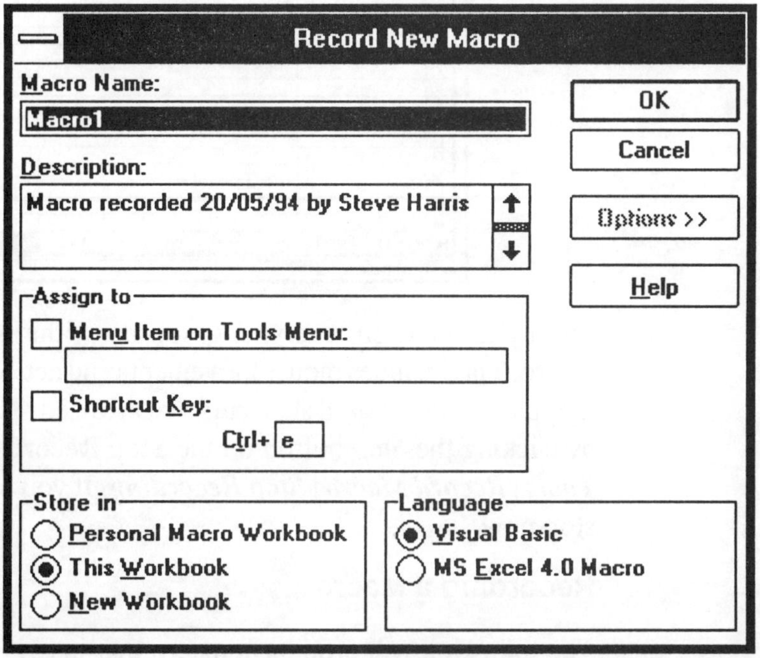

*Figure 10.2.
The expanded
dialogue box.*

This dialogue box allows further details about the macro to be defined, including how it should be activated and where it will be stored. The *Language* options allow you to record macros that are compatible with Excel 4.0, which may prove useful if you will be working with other Excel users who may not have upgraded their software. With the exception of the language choice, the details can be modified subsequently, although it is best to get them correct from the start.

After clicking the *OK* button, the Record New Macro dialogue box is removed from the screen and the Macro Record toolbar appears in its place. Also the *Recording* indicator appears on the left hand side of the status bar at the bottom of the screen. These features are shown in Figure 10.3.

Figure 10.3. Stop Recording toolbar and indicator.

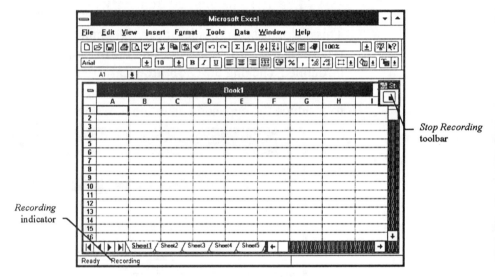

From this point on, everything you do within Excel is recorded into the macro. This includes mouse movements and actions, menu selections, as well as typing and keyboard shortcuts that are used. The recording is ended either by clicking the *Stop* button on the Stop Recording toolbar, or by selecting *Tools | Record Macro | Stop Recording*. If you have started recording, then stop now.

Recording a Macro

The following will produce a macro that inserts headings for four quarters into the spreadsheet, starting at the current cell location. It then emboldens the headings and right aligns them.

1   Close any existing workbooks that you may have open.

2   Click on the *New* button to create a new, blank workbook.

3   Select ***Tools | Record Macro | Record New Macro***.

4   Enter the name of the macro as ***Quarterly_Headings***. Note that an underscore is used to separate the two words – spaces are not allowed.

5   Enter the following description for the macro: **This macro inserts four emboldened, right-aligned quarterly headings**.

6   Click the *OK* button to start recording.

7   The procedure to record is quite straightforward.

   - Enter **QTR 1** into the current cell.

   - Click and drag the *Fill Handle* three columns to the right. If you started in cell A1, this means that you would drag across to D1.

   - Excel automatically fills the cells with **QTR 2**, **QTR 3** and **QTR 4**, leaving all four headings highlighted.

   - Click the *Bold* button $\boxed{\textbf{B}}$ once to embolden the text.

   - Click the *Align Right* button $\boxed{\equiv}$ once to right align the cells.

8   Stop the macro recorder by clicking the *Stop* button $\boxed{\blacksquare}$ on the Stop Recording toolbar.

9   The macro has now been recorded and stored in the current workbook, in a sheet called Module1.

10 Click on the *Save* button $\boxed{\blacksquare}$ and save the workbook in the STEPXL directory under the name **MAC_TEST**.

Writing Macros

Whilst the recording technique can be used for the majority of "speed-up" type macros, it does not lend itself well to certain tasks, and provides no way at all to access features such as custom dialogue boxes and the structured macro commands that allow looping and conditional macros to be produced. Thus in order to make the most of the macro language, it will be necessary to write certain macros without the assistance of the recorder. This is done by first selecting an existing module or creating a new module with *Insert | Macro | Module*, then entering the macro statements. All macro commands need to be placed between two special statements – "**Sub**" and "**End Sub**". These correspond to the beginning and end of the macro, and must be entered by you together with all of the other commands.

Examining Macro Code

The following displays the code for the *Quarterly_Headings* macro on-screen:

1   Ensure that the MAC_TEST workbook is open; if not use the *Open* button 🗁 to bring it into memory.

2   Click on the sheet tab for **Module1**.

3   The macro code for the *Quarterly_Headings* macro is displayed, preceded by a "Sub Quarterly_Headings()" command and followed by an "End Sub" statement, as shown in Figure 10.4.

Figure 10.4. Viewing macro code.

```
MAC_TEST.XLS
'
' Quarterly_Headings Macro
' This macro inserts four emboldened, right-aligned quarterly headings
'
'
Sub Quarterly_Headings()
    ActiveCell.FormulaR1C1 = "'Qtr 1"
    Selection.AutoFill Destination:=Range("A1:D1"), Type:= _
        xlFillDefault
    Range("A1:D1").Select
    Selection.Font.Bold = True
    With Selection
        .HorizontalAlignment = xlRight
        .VerticalAlignment = xlBottom
        .WrapText = False
        .Orientation = xlHorizontal
    End With
End Sub
```

Sheet14 / Sheet15 / Sheet16 \ **Module1** /

You can also see that the first five lines of the macro start with an apostrophe character. This indicates that these lines are *comments*, and Excel will not attempt to execute them. Instead they are there for your information, in this case showing the name and the description of the macro.

Executing a Macro

Once recorded or written, macros can be executed in a number of different ways. One of the simplest is to select *Tools | **Macro***, which produces the Macro dialogue box shown in Figure 10.5.

Using these options, any macros can be executed, edited, deleted or have its options changed as required.

Figure 10.5.
The Macro
dialogue box.

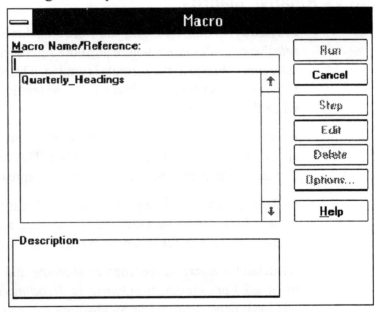

For example, to run the Quarterly_Headings macro:

1   Ensure MAC_TEST is open, or use the *Open* button 🖙 to bring it into memory if not.

2   Activate *Sheet 2* by clicking on its sheet tab at the bottom of the screen. This sheet should currently be blank.

3   Click in cell A1.

4   Select *Tools | Macro*.

5   Select the Quarterly_Headings entry from the *Macro Names/References* list and click on the *Run* button.

6   The macro code is now executed and the headings are inserted, exactly as they were recorded.

If this fails to work, or if the macro doesn't do quite what you expected, then go back to the walkthrough on recording the macro and try again.

Absolute Vs Relative Macros

Previously, in Chapter Eight, you were introduced to the idea of *absolute* and *relative* cell references, where absolute references remain fixed but relative references change as the formula is copied. This idea also extends to macros, with the differences between absolute and relative macros becoming obvious when they are executed.

- Absolute macros always execute at the same location, typically the location at which they were recorded. This makes them ideal for macros developed to support a specific spreadsheet or workbook.

- Relative macros execute at a location that is dependent on the current cell. This makes them ideal for automating common tasks, such as inserting text or formulae, formatting, printing etc.

By default a macro is recorded as absolute and so exact cell locations are recorded. For example, the *Quarterly_Headings* macro recorded previously will have been recorded as an absolute macro (unless you had previously reconfigured your software), so if it is executed at a different location it will not work:

1   Ensure MAC_TEST is open, or use the *Open* button [≥] to bring it into memory if not.

2   Activate *Sheet 3* by clicking on its sheet tab at the bottom of the screen. This sheet should currently be blank.

3   Click in cell A10.

4   Select *Tools | Macro* and select the Quarterly_Headings entry from the *Macro Names/References* list, then click on the *Run* button.

5   Excel attempts to execute the macro code, but fails when it tries to use the AutoFill feature, producing the dialogue box shown in Figure 10.6

Figure 10.6. Macro error message.

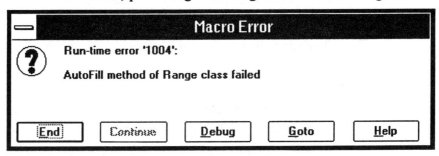

6   Click on the *End* button to terminate the macro.

If the macro is executed at the original location, even within another sheet, then it works perfectly:

1   With *Sheet 3* still active, click on cell A1.

2   Execute the macro using the *Tools | Macro* technique.

3   The macro code should execute correctly.

Choosing Between Absolute and relative Recording

In general you may find it preferable to record macros using relative references. For example, to record a relative macro that adds borders and shading to the current cell:

1   Active *Sheet 4* in the MAC_TEST workbook.

2   Select cells A1:D1.

3   Enable the macro recorder by selecting *Tools | Record Macro | Record New Macro*.

4   Enter the macro name as **BordersAndShading**, and the description as **This macro adds borders and shading to the current cell selection**.

5   Click the *OK* button to begin recording.

6   Enable relative recording by selecting *Tools | Record Macro | Use Relative References*. This is a toggle option; once selected, the menu option will have a small tick by its side to show that the feature is enabled.

7   The procedure to record is quite straightforward.

  • Select *Format | Cells*.

  • Click on the *Border* tab in the resulting dialogue box, and add a single border at the top, and a double border at the bottom of the selection.

  • Click on the *Patterns* tab and click on the down arrow to the right of the *Pattern* box. Select once of the patterns from the first three rows of the resulting list.

  • Click *OK* to close the Format Cells dialogue box.

8   Stop the macro recorder by clicking the *Stop* button ▣ on the Stop Recording toolbar.

9   The macro has now been recorded and stored in the current workbook, in a sheet called Module2.

10 Click on the *Save* button 💾 and save the workbook (remember that this saves the workbook under its existing name).

Having selected relative references in this way, the feature remains enabled until Excel is restarted, or you manually deselect the option.

To test the macro and ensure that it is in fact relative:

1   Activate *Sheet 1*, or any sheet that contains data.

2   Highlight the cells to be formatted.

3   Select *Tools | Macro*, highlight the BordersAndShading macro and click the *Run* button.

Exercise

> **1**   Record a macro, using absolute references, that copies the content of the current cell for three columns to the right, then inserts a summation of all four columns into the cell to the right of the last value. Test run the macro to ensure it works – remember you must be in the same location as was used for recording the macro.
>
> **2**   Record the same macro, but use relative references. Test the macro using the original, and different, locations.
>
> **3**   Compare the code for the two macros. What are the key differences?

Assigning a Keyboard Shortcut to a Macro

Running a macro through the Macro dialogue box is not a very efficient way of using this powerful facility, and it would be far better to use a shortcut key. The assignment of a shortcut key to a macro is as follows:

1   Ensure that MAC_TEST is open.

2   Select *Tools | Macro*, and highlight the Quarterly_Headings macro in the list.

3   Click the *Options* button to display the Macro Options dialogue box shown in Figure 10.7.

Figure 10.7.
Macro Options
dialogue box.

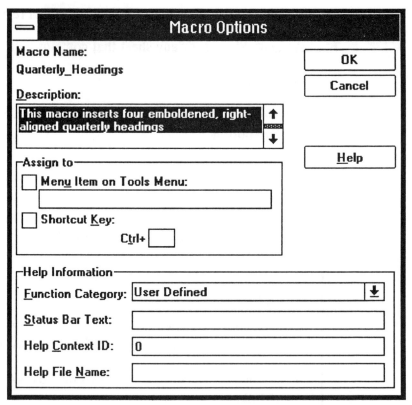

4 Click on the *Shortcut Key* box to check it, then click in the *Ctrl+* box and enter **Q**.

5 Click *OK*, then choose the *Close* button from the Macro dialogue box.

6 Activate *Sheet 5* and select cell A1.

7 Press CTRL+Q to run the macro

Assigning a Toolbar Button to a Macro

In addition to running macros through keyboard shortcuts, it is also useful to create a button on a toolbar that can be used to run a macro. This is not achieved through the Macro Options dialogue box, but through the Customize dialogue box instead.

1   Ensure MAC_TEST is open.

2   Activate *Sheet 6* and select cell A1.

3   Select *View | Toolbars* and click on the *Customize* button. The Customize
dialogue box appears as shown in Figure 10.8.

Figure 10.8.
Customize
dialogue box.

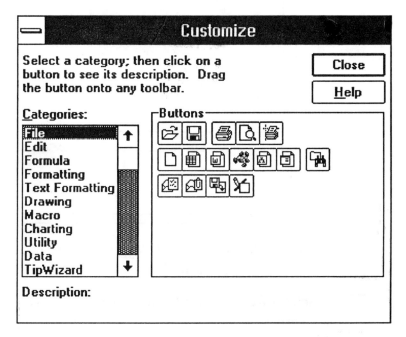

4   Scroll down the *Categories* list and highlight the Custom option, which
will be found at the bottom. The *Buttons* area will change to show a
selection of user-definable buttons.

5   Click and drag one of these buttons (the smiley face stands out well) onto
an existing toolbar. When you release the mouse button you are prompted
with the Assign Macro dialogue box, as shown in Figure 10.9.

Figure 10.9.
Assign Macro
dialogue box.

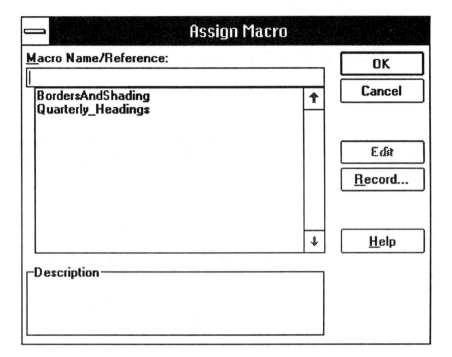

6   Click on the *BorderAndShading* entry, then click *OK*. The macro has now been assigned to the tool.

7   Select *Close* from the Customize dialogue box to return to the spreadsheet.

8   To test the assignment, click on the new button and the macro will be executed at the current cell.

Repositioning or Removing a Custom Button

1   Select *View | Toolbars* and click the *Customize* button to display the Customize dialogue box.

2   To move a button, click and drag it to its new location. This may be on the same toolbar or on a completely different one.

3   To remove a button, click and drag it away from the toolbars all together.

It is also possible to execute macros in several other ways. For example, a graphical object on a spreadsheet such as a line, rectangle or circle could be assigned to a macro using the *Tools | Assign Macro* command. Alternatively a complete custom dialogue box could be produced using the *Insert | Macro | Dialog* command. These topics are beyond the scope of this book, but are covered by a number of examples and demonstrations in the Excel documentation and help system.

Exercise

1   Assign a shortcut key combination of CTRL+B to the BordersAndShading macro.

2   Add a button to the standard toolbar to run the Quarterly_Headings macro. The button image to use is the speech bubble button from the custom category.

Summary

This chapter has served only as an introduction to the powerful area of macros in Excel. However, by the time you have reached this part of the book you should be thinking about writing simple macros to automate repetitive operations and to customise toolbars to better reflect the tasks you want to perform.

Self Test

1   What are the limitations on a macro name?

2   How can you tell if the name given to a macro is acceptable?

3   How can you delete a macro?

4   How can you obtain help on a macro command or statement?

5   If you record a macro into a named workbook and you save it to disk, what do you need to do if you want to run the macro the next time you start Excel?

6   Would you need to record or write a macro if you wanted to place a button on the Standard toolbar that inserted the current date into your worksheet?

7   How many different keyboard shortcuts can be used for running macros in Excel?

8   Is there a limit on the number of buttons that can be placed onto a toolbar?

9   How do you remove a button from a toolbar?

10   How could you allow a user to run a macro by clicking on a chart that had been inserted into the worksheet?

TWELVE
Working with Other Applications

Key Learning Points in This Chapter

- Importing graphs and pictures

- Linking to other files

- Transferring data with the Clipboard

- Using Dynamic Data Exchange to link with other applications

- Working with Object Linking & Embedding

Introduction

Among the more powerful features of Excel is the ability to incorporate information from other Windows applications within your spreadsheets and workbooks. This makes it easy to produce sophisticated and informative reports, proposals and other documentation. In fact you are only really limited by your imagination and the versatility of the other applications that you have.

There are a number of different ways to transfer information into Excel. Some are *static*, which means that once combined the data only changes if you edit it within Excel, whilst other techniques are *dynamic*, meaning that the copy of the data that you have in Excel is *linked* to the original application and can be updated if the original information is changed.

The techniques examined in this chapter comprise a mixture of static and dynamic methods. Furthermore they are complementary, which means you might use a combination of static and dynamic techniques when transferring data.

Inserting From Disk

You can take an existing data file from the disk and combine it with your spreadsheet. The file could be produced by another spreadsheet program, a word processor, a database or a graphics program. Once inserted, the flexibility is dependent on the type of information; graphics and images cannot be edited with Excel, so can only be changed within the original application. On the other hand, text and numbers handled in this way become a part of the spreadsheet, so may be edited with any of the features provided by Excel.

Clipboard

The clipboard allows you to use the *Copy* and *Paste* options under the *Edit* menu to transfer data between spreadsheets within Excel, or from one Windows application to another. It is a static technique, but is very quick and easy to use.

Dynamic Data Exchange (DDE)

DDE is similar to the Clipboard, except that it is dynamic. It may be used to transfer and link your spreadsheet figures into word processed documents, as it allows updates made to the figures to be automatically reflected in the other application. DDE can also be used between two spreadsheet files, or can be used to link information *into* Excel from another program.

Object Linking and Embedding (OLE)

OLE is the most flexible technique, as it may be either dynamic or static, and may be established through the *Edit* menu or the *Insert* menu options. Excel supports the OLE 2 standard, so is able to work with almost every other application that provides OLE features.

Loading Pictures from Disk

One of the easiest ways to incorporate pictures and images is to load an existing picture from the disk. This would typically have been produced with a drawing program such as Corel DRAW! or Lotus Freelance, but it may also be a graph from a spreadsheet such as Lotus 1-2-3.

File Formats

The file formats recognised by Excel are dependent upon the installation technique chosen. For example, using the Custom installation method it is possible to choose to omit specific file converters, which would prevent Excel from being to load files of that type.

If you had performed a complete installation when initially setting up the software, then Excel will have installed *filters* that recognise six specific file types, as shown below.

Windows MetaFile (WMF)	HP Graphics Language (HPGL)
Computer Graphics Metafile (CGM)	Encapsulated PostScript (EPS)
Tag Image File Format (TIFF)	PC Paint Brush (PCX)

However, in addition, Excel supports standard Windows file types such as BMPs and has permanent built-in support for files such as Lotus 1-2-3 PIC files, an can make use of graphics filters supplied with some other software, such as Microsoft Word. Therefore the list of recognisable file types is usually much more varied than you may first assume.

When you attempt to load a file from disk, Excel examines it to see if it is one of the recognised formats, even if the file does not have one of the standard extensions. If the file type is supported then the data will be loaded, otherwise an error message will be displayed.

Loading a Picture

Pictures are loaded into a document through the *Insert | Picture* commands. The dialogue box produced when these commands are selected is shown in Figure 12.1:

Figure 12.1.
The Picture
dialogue box.

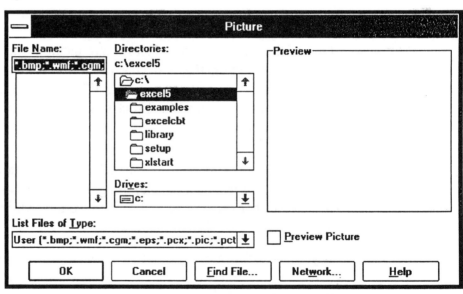

The *List Files of Type* option currently specifies "User", followed by a list of file extensions that will be recognised.. The arrow to the right of this text can be clicked to drop down a list of specific graphics file formats, together with their default extensions. If you know that you are looking for a specific file type, such as a Lotus PIC file then the "Lotus 1-2-3 Graphics" option could be selected instead, thus limiting the list of displayed files to those with a PIC extension only.

The *Preview Picture* check box can be selected if you want to see a simplified image of the picture as you highlight its name in the list. This is useful if you know what the picture looks like, but can't quite remember what it was called or where it was stored.

Excel is supplied with no graphics files of its own, and therefore the following example shows how to load one of the standard Windows graphics files – WINLOGO.BMP. If you have other applications, such as PowerPoint or Word installed, check to see if they have *Clipart* or graphics available. If so you may want to use these files instead of the WINLOGO image.

1   Close any existing workbooks. Remember that you can close everything by holding the SHIFT key down, then selecting *File | Close All*.

2   Create a new workbook by clicking the *New Workbook* button.

3   Click in cell C5 on *Sheet 1* to make it active.

4   Select *Insert | Picture*.

5   Change the directory to C:\WINDOWS or similar. This is the directory in which Windows was installed.

6   A list of files with BMP extensions should be displayed. If not, see if there is another directory on your disk that contains graphics files.

7   Scroll down and select WINLOGO.BMP and click *OK*.

8   Save the workbook as PICBOOK1.

Positioning, Sizing and Formatting Pictures

Having loaded the picture into the document it can be positioned, sized and formatted as required.

Positioning Pictures

Positioning is controlled by clicking and dragging the picture to the desired location. Furthermore, if the underlying cells are moved, the picture moves with them. This behaviour can be changed if necessary.

Sizing Pictures

Sizing is controlled with the mouse, using special *sizing handles* that are displayed on the picture when it is selected, as shown in Figure 12.2.

Figure 12.2.
Picture sizing handles.

Sizing handles

To resize the picture, first click within the image to select it. Once selected it will be shown with 8 separate handles around its perimeter, as shown in Figure 12.2. Clicking and dragging any of these handles allows the picture to be resized in the direction you drag. Dragging a corner handle allows both height and width to be changed simultaneously, whilst the side handles stretch the picture in just one direction. If you want to ensure that the *aspect ratio* (height : width) is maintained, hold the SHIFT key down as you drag a corner handle.

Formatting Pictures

A limited amount of formatting is provided for pictures loaded from disk through the *Format | Object* command. This only becomes available once the picture has been selected. A shortcut for this command is to double-click the picture in the workbook., or use the right mouse button to display the shortcut menu.

However selected, the Format Object dialogue box appears as shown in Figure 12.3.

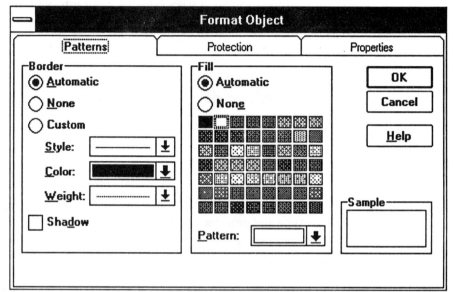

Figure 12.3.
Format Object
dialogue box.

The *Patterns* tab shows options that relate to the colour and style of the fill pattern and border of the picture. Since these are general-purpose options, they may or may not have an effect on the displayed image, depending on the file type. For example, changing the *Fill* options for a bitmap has no effect, but changing them for a Windows MetaFile causes the background to change.

The *Protection* tab shows a single option – *Locked*. This dictates whether the image is editable when the workbook or sheet is protected. By default, *Locked* is checked but the sheet is not protected, so this setting has no effect. However, if you select **Tools | Protection | Protect Sheet** or **Protect Workbook** then you will find that the graphic cannot be selected, moved or changed in any way.

The *Properties* tab displays options relating to the pictures ability to be automatically sized, positioned and printed. The default is that the picture is moved if the underlying cells are moved, but will not be resized. Other options allow the picture to be moved and sized or to remain static. A further checkbox allows you to define whether the picture should be printed when the sheet is printed.

Exercise

> **1**   Insert the LEAVES.BMP picture into a blank sheet in
>   PICBOOK1. This image can be found in the \WINDOWS
>   directory.
>
> **2**   Resize the Leaves picture so that it occupies approximately half
>   its original size, maintaining the original aspect ratio.

The Clipboard

The Clipboard is used to transfer information between two different locations, which could be in the same application or in totally different applications. You can think of the Clipboard as a general-purpose storage area, which can hold any type and amount of information from your application. Once information is placed onto the Clipboard, it remains there until you exit Windows, or until something else is placed onto the Clipboard instead.

- Information is transferred *to* the Clipboard using the *Edit | Cut* and *Edit | Copy* commands. Cut removes the original information, whereas Copy duplicates it.

- Information is transferred *from* the Clipboard using the *Edit | Paste* command. Paste can be used any number of times in succession as the data stays on the Clipboard until it is replaced.

Using the Clipboard Within Excel

The following will duplicate the bitmap inserted previously.

1   Ensure that PICBOOK1 is open, and click on the tab for Sheet 1 to make it visible.

2   Click on the Winlogo picture to select it.

3   Select *Edit | Copy* to copy the picture to the clipboard.

4   Click on a cell just below the picture – this will be the top left location of the picture when you paste it.

5   Select *Edit | Paste* to produce another copy of the picture.

6   Click to the right of the second picture and select *Edit | Paste* again to produce a third copy of the image.

You can repeat this as many times as you like. The picture remains on the clipboard until something else is cut or copied.

Using the Clipboard with Another Application

In addition to working within an application, the Clipboard can be used to transfer information between applications, even applications of different types. For example, it is quite possible to use the Clipboard to transfer a picture from Paintbrush into Excel.

1   Switch to Program Manager and start Paintbrush.

2   Create a simple image in Paintbrush.

3   Click on the selection tool at the top right of the Paintbrush toolbar

4   Drag a rectangle around the section of your image that you want to copy.

5   Select *Edit | Copy* to copy the image to the Clipboard.

6   Close Paintbrush.

7   Switch back to Excel and select a cell on Sheet 1 on PICBOOK1..

8   Select *Edit | Paste* to transfer the picture into the sheet.

The selected portion of the image is brought into Excel and can be positioned and sized in the same way as a loaded picture.

Exercise

1   Transfer the range A1:F10 of TRENDY_M.XLS into Paintbrush using the Copy and paste commands.

Dynamic Data Exchange (DDE)

The Clipboard techniques produce a non-changing or *static* copy of the original data within your document. If you want a dynamic copy, that is linked to original data in another application then you need to use a different technique. One of the options for this is to *use Dynamic Data Exchange*, although there are some other methods available as well.

The easiest way to create a DDE link is via the *Edit | Paste Special* command, which produces the dialogue box shown in Figure 12.4. In fact this dialogue box is also used when working with Object Linking and Embedding (OLE) techniques as well which is discussed later in this chapter.

Figure 12.4.
Paste Special
dialogue box.

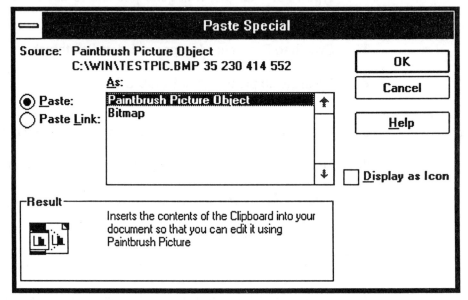

In this case you can see that the data currently on the Clipboard is a Paintbrush picture called TESTPIC. The precise options available may differ with other data types.

Creating a Link into Excel

The creation of a DDE link is very similar to the copy and paste technique used for the Clipboard. The first example uses Paintbrush to illustrate linking data *into* Excel:

1   Switch to Program Manager and run Paintbrush.

2   Create a simple image and save it to the disk as LINK2.BMP. You *must* save the picture in order for DDE to work.

3   Using the selection tool, highlight an area of your image and copy it to the Clipboard.

4   Without closing Paintbrush, switch to Excel and click on the tab for *Sheet 2*.

5   Choose *Edit | Paste Special*.

6   Change the type of data to *Bitmap*, then click on the *Paste Link* button.

7   Click on the *OK* button to paste the image and return to the sheet.

8   Save the workbook under the existing name.

Updating Linked Data

Having created the link, any changes to the original file will be automatically reflected in the linked copy.

1   Switch to Paintbrush, leaving Excel open with your workbook loaded.

2   Make a change to your image (LINK2.BMP) within the area that you copied to the Clipboard.

3   Switch back to Excel and you will see that the change has been automatically made to the copy of the image in your document.

Changing a Link

Having made the change to the original picture, you will have seen that there was a small delay when the image was updated in Excel. As you use more and more DDE links between applications you may find that the time taken to update them becomes extended, and could slow the entire system down quite considerably.

Therefore you may choose to change the type of the link from an *Automatic* link to a *Manual* link. As you would expect, the automatic link reflects any changes to the original information immediately, whereas the manual link requires that you choose the *Update Now* button from the Links dialogue box to make the changes appear. This dialogue box is produced with the *Edit | Links* command, and is shown in Figure 12.5.

Figure 12.5. The Links dialogue box.

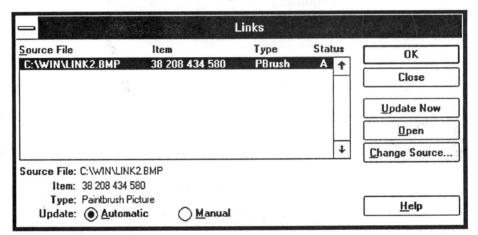

The *Automatic* and *Manual* option buttons at the bottom of the dialogue box define the link type, whilst the buttons to the right are used to manage the link. Note that if there are multiple links within a document it is only the highlighted one that is affected if you change any settings. If more than one link is to be modified then CTRL click each of them before changing the settings, as this allows multiple selections to be made.

1 Choose *Edit | Links* to display the dialogue box.

2 Ensure the link to Paintbrush is selected.

3 Click on the *Manual* option button, then click OK.

4 Switch to Paintbrush, leaving Excel open with your workbook loaded.

5 Make a change to your image (LINK2.BMP) within the area that you copied to the Clipboard.

6 Switch back to Excel. You will find that the change you have just made in Paintbrush is not yet reflected in the workbook.

7 Select *Edit | Links* again and choose the *Update Now* button.

8 The document image is updated to show the recent changes.

Creating a Link From Excel

In many cases you will find that you use DDE not for linking data into Excel, but for linking worksheet information into another application, such as Microsoft Word. This allows you to easily create high-impact reports and proposals based around spreadsheet data, and still be secure in the knowledge that any changes to the spreadsheet will be reflected in the word processed document.

This example shows how you can link between Excel and Word. If you have a different Windows word processor then you may need to use some different keystrokes or menu selections, but it is unlikely that there will be any substantial differences.

1 Close PICBOOK1, saving the changes that you have made, then open TRENDY_M.XLS. Remember it is not strictly necessary to close the existing workbook – but it is likely to speed things up.

2 Highlight the cell range A1:F10, in other words the entire plan.

3 Select *Edit | Copy* to transfer the data to the clipboard.

4 Switch to Program Manager and start Microsoft Word, or your chosen word processing application. It should start with a blank document.

5 Enter the following text:

> **MEMO TO ALL SALES STAFF**
>
> **Here is the sales forecast for the coming months. Let's all pull together to ensure we make target.**

6 Press enter twice to insert some blank lines.

7   Choose *Edit | Paste Special*. The dialogue box shown in Figure 12.6 will
be displayed. Notice the similarity with the Paste Special dialogue box in
Excel.

*Figure 12.6.
The Paste
Special dialogue
box in Word.*

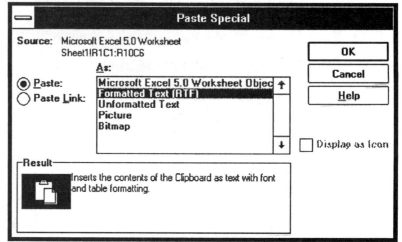

8   Click on the *Paste* Link option button, then click on *OK*. The data is
linked into the Word document as a *table*.

9   Press ENTER twice more to insert blank lines beneath the table.

10   Enter the following:

   **As you can see, the total sales figure of XXX is somewhat
   higher than previous quarters.**

11   The XXX is to be replaced with a linked reference to cell F10 of the
spreadsheet, so switch back to Excel, click on cell F10 and select *Edit |
Copy*.

12   Switch back to Word and delete the XXX indicator.

13   With the insertion point between the words "of" and "is", select *Edit |
Paste Special*, change the type of data to *Unformatted Text*, click on the
Paste Link option then click on the *OK* button to insert the value.

14   Switch back to Excel and change the value in cell B9 from **1800** to **2000**.
The plan is recalculated and the linked data updated in the Word
document.

15 Save your document as FCASTDDE.DOC, then close Word.

The above example has shown that the use of DDE is not limited to producing tabular type layouts; it is quite possible, and often rather useful, to link data into the middle of a paragraph in the word processor. Also notice the use of the *Unformatted Text* option when linking into the paragraph. This ensures that any formatting applied to the paragraph of text is also applied to the linked data, making it blend neatly into the document.

Exercise

1 Open the TRENDY_M plan and link cells A10:F10 into the Microsoft Write application that is supplied with Windows.

2 Link cell F10 of the TRENDY_M plan into a new workbook in Excel. Notice the different options you are provided with during this process.

Object Linking & Embedding (OLE)

The third data transfer technique is to use Object Linking and Embedding. This is the most flexible technique as it provides a similar set of features to the Clipboard and DDE combined. However, OLE is not as widely supported as the Clipboard or DDE, although all of the Microsoft Office applications (Excel, Word, PowerPoint etc.) support OLE fully.

The two main ways to include OLE information in an Excel workbook are through the use of the *Edit | Paste Special* command, and through the *Insert | Object* command.

Having created the object it will look almost the same as if it had been created with the Clipboard or with DDE. It is only when you start to change the data that the differences become apparent.

Pasting an Object

1 Switch to Program Manager and run Paintbrush.

2   Create a simple image. Unlike DDE, there is no need to save the image to the disk.

3   Using the selection tool, highlight an area of your image and copy it.

4   Switch to Excel and open the PICBOOK1 workbook.

5   Click on the tab for *Sheet 3*, then click in cell C5. As mentioned before, this defines the position for the data to be inserted.

6   Select *Edit | Paste Special*.

7   Ensure the type is *Paintbrush Picture Object*, then click the *Paste* button.

8   Click on the *OK* button to paste the image and return to the worksheet.

It is also possible to create a linked object, by saving the original file before copying the data, then choosing the *Paste Link* option. This will behave in much the same way as a link created using the DDE techniques discussed previously.

Inserting an Object

Rather than having to manually launch the application supplying the data, this technique allows you to use the features of Excel to start the program for you.

1   With PICBOOK1 open, click on the tab for *Sheet 4*, then select cell C5 again as the location for the object that will be inserted.

2   Select *Insert | Object*.

3   Scroll down the *Object Type* list and select *Paintbrush Picture*.

4   Click on *OK* and Excel will automatically launch Paintbrush.

5   Draw a simple image.

6   Select *File | Exit & Return to PICBOOK1*.

7   A dialogue box asks whether the image should be updated. Click on *Yes* to ensure that the image is transferred into your worksheet.

8   On returning to Excel you will find the image has been inserted into the document. As with any picture it can be positioned and sized as required.

As you will see, the Object dialogue box lists many different object types, some of which are supplied with Windows (such as *Paintbrush Picture*) whilst others relate to other applications (such as a *Microsoft Word 6.0 Document*).

Editing an Object

An object can be changed or updated very easily. Double clicking the object within the document causes the original (source) application to be executed and the data loaded into it. Having completed the changes the *File | Exit* command will return you to Excel.

1   Double-click the inserted Paintbrush Picture.

2   Once Paintbrush has loaded, make some changes to the picture.

3   Select *File | Exit & Return to PICBOOK1* to return to Excel.

Exercise

1   Use the *Insert | Object* command to insert a *Paintbrush Picture* into your worksheet.

2   Experiment with the other object types available. Remember that these are dependent on the other Windows applications that you have installed on your PC.

Summary

The data transfer features of Excel are extremely powerful, and this chapter has only begun to demonstrate what can be achieved through their use.

When working with a suite of Windows applications, such as the Microsoft Office products, these features guarantee that the different programs can efficiently transfer data to one another with a minimum of effort. For example, if you had created a financial plan spreadsheet in Excel, either the Clipboard, DDE or OLE could be used to transfer that information into Word, PowerPoint or Project.

When choosing between these techniques remember their key differences. The Clipboard provides a once-only transfer which will not be automatically updated under any circumstances. DDE allows the data to be updated either automatically or manually, but can slow the system down. OLE provides an easy way to edit the information, but does have a tendency to substantially increase the size of the document files, thus consuming more disk space.

Self Test

1   How many graphic file formats can Excel recognise?

2   What command is used to insert a picture into an Excel worksheet?

3   How can you preview a picture prior to inserting it into a document?

4   What is the difference between using a corner handle and a side handle when resizing a picture?

5   How can you maintain the aspect ratio of a picture when resizing it?

6   How long does information remain on the Clipboard?

7   What does DDE stand for and what is the benefit of using this technique?

8   When working with a DDE link, what is the difference between a *manual* and an *automatic* link?

9   What does OLE stand for and how does it differ from DDE?

10 How do you edit an image that has been inserted into a plan as an OLE object?

APPENDIX A
Answers to Self Tests

Chapter One

1   What is the name of the suite of programs that includes Microsoft Word, Excel and PowerPoint?

The suite of programs is known as Microsoft Office, and is available in two versions. Microsoft Office Standard includes Word, Excel, PowerPoint and a licence to use Mail on the workstation. Microsoft Office Professional includes all of these plus Microsoft Access, one of the most powerful and flexible database system for Windows.

2   What does the TipWizard do?

The TipWizard offers alternative ways of performing a particular task in Excel. It is interactive and reports its suggestion at the top of the screen whilst you are working. The TipWizard is activated by clicking on the TipWizard button within Excel.

3   How much memory is needed in the PC to run Excel, and how much more is recommended?

Excel requires at least 4MB of memory to run. However, you system will be very slow with only this amount of memory and thus at lest 8MB is recommended. If you are running other Windows applications then performance will be greatly enhanced by increasing memory to 16MB.

4   Which versions of DOS and Windows are required to run Excel?

Excel requires DOS version 3.1 or higher, and requires Windows version 3.1 or higher. Both of these are minimums, and you may find advantages to using more modern versions such as DOS 6.2 and Windows 3.11.

5   What is the maximum length of a DOS filename?

A DOS filename is limited in length to 8 characters, with an optional 3 character extension. However, the extension is usually reserved for use by the application, so that it can identify its own data files.

6   Which of the following filenames are valid?

REPORT.XLS
NEW PLAN.XLS
INFORMATION

REPORT.XLS is a valid filename as the first part of the name is only 6 characters, and the 3 character extension correctly identifies the file as an Excel file.

NEW PLAN.XLS is invalid as it contains a space, even though the total number of characters is within limits. Therefore this would be rejected by the software.

INFORMATION is also invalid as the name is too long. This could be made into a valid name by separating the name into an 8 character section and a 3 character section – INFORMAT.ION. However, this is likely to cause problems as your application may not automatically recognise this file and therefore this approach is not recommended.

7   How do you start Windows?

Once installed, Windows is executed by typing WIN at the DOS prompt. If this appears not to work then you may need to check the PATH statement for DOS to ensure that Windows is correctly set up. More information on this is provided in the Windows and DOS documentation.

8 What is an icon?

An icon is a small graphical image that is used to represent an application, a data file, a directory, or some special program feature in the Windows environment. Icons are a key part of any graphical user interface.

9 How do you run an application from within Windows?

To run an application you must first find its icon. This may be displayed on screen, or may be contained in one of the minimised program groups. Having located the icon, double-click it using the left mouse button to run the program. You can also use the *File | Run* command to run an application if you know the name of the program and its location on the disk.

10 Suggest two ways of switching between applications in Windows.

Pressing ALT+TAB allows you to cycle through the open applications. A box with the application name is displayed in the middle of the screen and when you want to go to an application you release the keys.

Pressing ALT+ESC has a similar effect, but displays the whole window which makes it a slower method.

Chapter Two

1 With Windows running, what is required to load Excel?

Excel is loaded by double-clicking the left mouse button whilst it is pointing to the Excel Icon on the desktop. It may be necessary to first access the group in which Excel is located - for example, Microsoft Office, by double-clicking on that icon first to display the window that contains the Excel icon.

2 What is the "active cell" and how do you change it?

The active cell is the cell into which data will be entered or for cells already containing information it is the one you can see the contents of on the formula bar. The active cell has a bold border and when a new workbook is opening it will be on cell A1 on sheet 1. You can change the active cell either by moving the mouse pointer to another cell and clicking or by pressing the directional arrow keys.

3   When you start Excel how many sheets are available in a workbook?

Excel presents 16 sheets in a workbook, although the maximum number of sheets that you can place in a workbook is 256. This could be a combination of worksheets, chart sheets, macro sheets etc.

4   Which toolbars are displayed by default when Excel is started?

Excel displays the Standard toolbar and the Formatting toolbar by default. The buttons on these toolbars can be customised to suit your own requirements and you can choose to display different toolbars when you start up Excel.

5   Describe two ways of displaying the Chart toolbar.

Clicking the right mouse button whilst the pointer is over the grey area of the toolbars at the top of the screen displays the shortcut menu for toolbars and Chart can be selected. Alternatively the *View* | *Toolbars* command may be used and the Chart box checked.

6   What is required to make the Chart toolbar "float"?

The mouse pointer is positioned somewhere on the toolbar, but not actually on a button. You can now click and drag the toolbar to another location on the screen. You can also resize the toolbar to different shape if necessary.

7   What is required to re-anchor the Chart toolbar?

Double-clicking on the Chart toolbar title returns it to a fixed position, below the Formatting toolbar.

8   Describe two ways of hiding the Chart toolbar.

The *View* | *Toolbars* command may be used to clear the Chart box.

Alternatively, click on the right mouse button with the mouse pointer somewhere on the toolbars. This will produce a list of toolbars and the Chart option may be cleared.

9   How would you get help on the *File | Print* command?

You can click on the *Help Tool* button and then select *File | Print* and you will immediately access help on that command. Alternatively you can select *File | Print* but **before** releasing the mouse button press F1 which will access the appropriate help screen. Finally you can use the Help menu to search for help on printing.

10   What happens to the mouse pointer when the Help tool is activated?

A large question mark is displayed beside the mouse pointer. This indicates that any command that you access will not be executed, but help will be supplied on it.

Chapter Three

1   On which toolbar are the *Bold* and *Italic* buttons located?

These buttons are both located on the Formatting toolbar.

2   What name is given to the small square on the bottom right corner of the cell border?

This is referred to as the *fill handle* and is used for extending a series across a row or column.

3   How would you enter the days of the week in adjacent cells across a row?

Type in the day you want to begin with in a cell and the next day in an adjacent cell. Select both cells and then click on the fill handle and drag down or across the required range and the days will automatically be entered into the cells.

4   How can you edit the contents of a cell from within the cell?

Either by double clicking on the cell or by clicking once and then pressing F2 will allow you to edit the contents of a cell from within the cell as opposed to on the formula bar.

5   What is the effect of applying the *AutoFit* command to a range of cells.

AutoFit takes the cell with the most characters in the range and increases the column width to display the contents.

6   What is the first character of any formula?

All formulae in Excel must be preceded by an equals sign (=).

7   What results would the following formulae return?

    =8-2/3   would return 7.333333
    =(8-2)/3   would return 2
    =8-(2/3)   would return 7.333333
    =((8-2)/3) would return 2

8   What is meant by a *relative relationship* in the context of copying a formula from one cell to another?

A relative relationship is one that adjusts when the formula is copied. In other words if the formula =B2*B3 is entered into cell B4 and is then copied into cells C4 and D4, the references will change to be =C2*C3 and =D2*D3 respectively. The relationship that was established in the original formula is retained.

9   How do you total the values in a range of cells?

If the total is required in an adjacent cell to the range the *AutoSum* button can be clicked and it will suggest the range to total. If the range is incorrect you can insert the correct one. Alternatively you can use the SUM function to specify the range of cells you want to total.

10 How do you update a file on disk after you have made some changes to it?

Clicking on the *Save* button on the Standard toolbar will update the file on disk using the current name. Alternatively you can select *File | Save*.

Chapter Four

1 To what accuracy are numbers displayed by default?

By default numbers are displayed in a *General* format which means that as many decimal places as will fit into the cell will be shown.

2 To what accuracy are numbers calculated by default?

Calculation is, by default, performed to 15 decimal places.

3 What are the disadvantages of using the General format?

The general format can be untidy in that cells can have different numbers of decimal places, making the values hard to read.

4 What are the differences between Accounting and Currency formats?

The Accounting format option includes spaces so that the currency symbol is aligned to the left of the cell, regardless of the cell width, whilst Currency displays the currency symbol immediately to the left of the first digit of the value.

5 What effect does the *Precision As Displayed* option on the *Calculation* tab of the Options dialogue box have on the worksheet calculations?

When a cell is formatted it is only the display that changes and the calculation is still performed to 15 decimal places. The *Precision As Displayed* option allows you to change the value to the displayed number of decimal places so that future calculations will use the fixed number of decimals.

6   How do you define a format that shows positive numbers with commas separating the thousands and four decimal places?

You need to select the range to be formatted and then click on the *Comma* button to indicate that you want commas to separate thousands. Then use the *Increase Decimals* button to increase the number of decimal places to 4.

7   How can you amend this format to display currency symbols as well?

Click on the *Currency* button which will add the currency symbol, but will reduce the number of decimal places to 2. You must then use the *Increase Decimal* button to return the number of decimal places to 4.

8   In addition to using the *Borders* button, how can you apply a border to a range of cells?

You can use the ***Format | Cells | Borders*** command to specify borders for selected cells.

9   What is the easiest way to apply a border around every cell in a range, rather than an outline around the entire range?

An option from within the *Borders* button is ⊞ which outlines each cell as opposed to the outer edge of the range.

10   How can you format a cell to show reversed-out text, i.e. white letters on a black background?

The *Color* and *Font Color* buttons can be used to change the colour of the cell and the contents of the cell respectively. Selecting a font colour of white and cell colour of black has the effect of formatting the cell to display reversed-out text.

Chapter Five

1   Suggest two ways of printing the entire plan.

Providing you do not need to change any of the print specifications you can print a plan by clicking on the *Print* button on the Standard toolbar. Alternatively you can select *File | Print* .

2   What is required to print pages 2 and 6 of a plan?

You must access the Print dialogue box with *File | Print* and from within there you can click on the *Pages* button and then enter **2,6** to indicated that only pages 2 and 6 are required.

3   How can you print a selected range of a plan?

Make sure that the range to print is highlighted and then select *File | Print* and click on the *Selection* option.

4   What is the quickest way to access Print Preview?

Clicking on the *Print Preview* button is the quickest way to access Print Preview.

5   How can you see the margin size as you adjust it?

As you move the margins the actual margin size is displayed at the bottom left of the screen.

6   How do you clear the automatic page breaks?

Select *Tools | Options* and on the *View* tab clear the *Automatic Page Breaks* box.

7   How can you reduce the size of a plan to fit on fewer pages?

From within the Page Setup dialogue box click on the *Page* tab. In the *Scaling* section you can either specify the percentage of normal size that you want to make the printout, or you can click the *Fit to* button and specify the number of pages in terms of width and height that you want the range to be printed on.

8   What is required to create a customised header?

From within the Page Setup dialogue box click on the *Header/Footer* tab. Click on *Custom Header* which produces a dialogue box into which you can enter customised header information.

9   What must you take into account when printing a range having set print titles?

You must not include the print titles in the print range. If you do they will be printed twice.

10   How do you print the formulae behind the values in a range?

Select *Tools | Options* and select the *View* tab. Click the *Formulas* checkbox which will display the formulae in the cells and will widen the cells in order that you can see the formulae. The range may now be printed in the usual way.

Chapter Six

1   What sheet types does Excel recognise as part of a workbook?

Excel recognises six different types of sheet - Worksheet, Chart sheet, Visual Basic Module, Dialog, Excel 4.0 macro sheet and Excel 4.0 International macro sheet.

2   How do you change the sheet tab label?

With the mouse pointer on the tab label click on the right mouse button. Select *Rename* and type in a new name for the sheet. Alternatively you can select *Format | Sheet | Rename*.

3   How do you group a series of sheets?

Click on the first sheet that you want to group, hold down the SHIFT key and click on the last sheet to be grouped. All sheets in the range will be grouped.

4   What tasks can be performed whilst sheets are grouped?

You can enter text and formulae that will be entered into the corresponding cells of all grouped sheets, you can format cells and ranges and you can hide or delete grouped sheets.

5   How do you ungroup sheets?

Click on one of the grouped tabs with the right mouse button and select *Ungroup Sheets*.

6   How do you display multiple sheets on the screen together?

You must select *Window | New* for as many sheets as you want to display. Select *Window | Arrange | Tile* to see all the windows on the screen together and then click on a different sheet tab in each window.

7   What is the format of a cell reference that references a cell in another sheet in the same workbook?

The format of the cell reference is:

=SHEET REFERENCE!CELL REFERENCE,

For example:

=SHEET3!B7-SHEET2!B7

8   What is the format of a cell reference that references a cell in a sheet in another workbook?

The format of the cell reference is:

=[FILENAME.XLS]SHEET REFERENCE!CELL REFERENCE,

For example:

=[BUDGET.XLS]SHEET3!B7-SHEET2!B7

If the workbook is in a different directory, the full path will also be specified.

9   What happens if you close a file without saving it first?

Excel will prompt you as to whether you want to save the file before closing. If you reply *Yes* the file will be saved and then closed. If you reply *No* the file will be closed without saving.

10 What happens when you open a workbook that contains links to another file?

A message is displayed asking if you want to update the links. If you reply *Yes* the links are updated and if you reply *No* the file is opened using the values it was saved with.

Chapter Seven

1   If you change the data from which the graph was created, will the chart reflect the changes made?

Yes, a chart is a graphical representation of the data in your worksheet and changing the data will automatically update the chart.

2   What is the difference between activating and selecting a chart?

Selecting a chart, which is achieved by single clicking somewhere in the chart area allow you to move, copy, delete and resize it. Activating on the other hand, which is achieved by double-clicking somewhere in the chart area allows you to edit various elements of the chart.

3   Can you change the format of a data series when a chart is selected?

No, a chart must be activated before a data series can be reformatted.

4   What is a data series as opposed to a data point? How do you select a data point in a chart?

A data point is a single point on a chart that has a specific value, whereas a data series represents a single row or column of data made up of related data points.

5   Can you draw three dimensional charts in Excel and in which step of the Chart Wizard would you select this option?

Yes and this is selected in step two of the Chart Wizard under chart types.

6   How can you add a legend and titles to a chart after you have completed step 5 of the Chart Wizard?

Activate the chart by double clicking on it and then select *Insert | Legend or Insert | Titles*.

7   What are the different ways of adding new data to a chart?

You can copy and paste data from any open worksheet in any workbook onto a graph. You must use the *Paste Special* option. If you are adding data to a chart from the same worksheet that the chart is on you can select the range and drag it onto the chart.

8   What are tickmarks and gridlines?

Tickmarks indicate the scaling points on the axis and gridlines are lines that go across or down the chart from the tickmarks.

9   How would you add a data label to a data point?

Activate the chart and then click on a data point to select it. With the mouse pointer on the selected data point click the right mouse button and select *Insert Data Labels*. You can then choose to display the label or the value for that data point. If you do not select a particular data point you will insert data labels for all data points.

10   How would you remove a data point from a graph?

You must remove the data from the worksheet so that it is not in the plotted range.

Chapter Eight

1 What constitutes an absolute cell reference and what are the options?

An absolute cell reference is one that remains fixed when copied to other cells. There are three options. A cell reference can be fully fixed which means both the row and column part of the reference are preceded with a dollar sign - for example, $B$7. Only the row part of the reference may be fixed - for example, B$7 or only the column part may be fixed - for example, $B7.

2 What function key can you use to make a cell reference absolute?

Pressing F4 with the insertion point somewhere on or immediately after a cell reference will insert the dollar signs. Pressing it repeatedly changes the setting from fully relative to row fixed, column fixed and fully fixed.

3 Why is it advantageous to display growth rates in a separate area of a plan as opposed to embedding them in a formula?

Changing growth rates and other factors when they are embedded in formulae is often a two step procedure as the first cell has to be edited and then this might need to be copied to other cells. In addition it is better model design to be able to see the growth rates etc. as opposed to having them embedded in formulae.

4 What is the difference between one-way and two-way data tables?

A one-way data table has a single input variable, but may have multiple output cells, whereas a two-way data table has two input variables, but is restricted to a single output cell.

5 What must the range of a data table include?

The range must include all the input data and the reference or references to the output cells.

6   Explain how a data table actually works.

The specified input cell or cells are replaced by the input variables entered into the table and the entire worksheet is repetitively recalculated for each variable. Only when all the calculation is complete are the results displayed in the table.

7   How can you test that the results of a data table are correct?

There are two ways to test the validity of a data table. If you enter an input variable, or variables in the case of a two-way table, into the worksheet the result cell should be the same as it is in the table. Another test is to include the data that you have in your worksheet in the table so you can check it is the same when the table has been calculated.

8   How can you prevent a table recalculating with the rest of the worksheet?

Under *Tools | Options | Calculation* there is an option to put calculation on *Automatic Except Tables* which means that the rest of the worksheet will be recalculated, but not the data tables unless you press F9 to manually recalculate them.

9   When deciding what to use as input and output variables what should you consider?

It is important to ensure that there is a relationship between the input variables and the output cells as without this the results of the table will be meaningless.

10   Can you change the data in a calculated data table?

No, the data is protected and if you attempt to overwrite one of the results, an error message will be displayed. You can, however, select all the results and delete them.

Chapter Nine

1 What do you do if the range suggested by AutoSum is not what you require?

You can click on the *cross* button to cancel the operation or you can replace the suggested selection with the range you require.

2 What must you be careful about when specifying a range to average?

The AVERAGE function ignores blank cells and cells containing text. If therefore you have some blank cells that you want to have included in the average calculation you must ensure they contain a zero value.

3 What is the effect of the INT function and give an example of when it might be useful.

The INT function truncates any decimal points that are attached to a value. An example of when this might be useful is when calculating the number of salesmen you are going to use for a project. You do not want half a salesman, and even if the result had .8 on the decimals you still cannot afford an additional salesman so you want the result truncated to the lower integer value regardless of the value of the decimals.

4 What is the difference between rounding a range to two decimal places with the ROUND function and using the Format command?

Using the ROUND function actually changes the value in the cell and the rounded value will be used for all calculations, whereas formatting the cell only affects the display and the actual value used for calculations retains the full degree of accuracy.

5 Give an example of when you might use the ABS function.

The ABS function returns the absolute value of a negative value. This might be useful when calculating overdraft repayments when you would want to use the negative cash flow figure as a positive value in the overdraft calculation.

Given the worksheet below, how would you calculate the following: (Assume you are entering formulae in cells A10 through A15).

	A	B	C	D
1	1	8	15	4
2	-2	-4	0	-6
3	1000	500	700	900
4	95	180	360	290
5				
6	100			

6   If the highest value in row 1 is more than 15, multiply A6 by 10, otherwise multiply cell A6 by 5.

=IF(MIN(A1:D1>15),A6*10,A6*5)

7   If there is a positive value in row 2 return the message *"too high"*, otherwise report the total value of the row as an absolute value.

=IF(MAX(A2:D2)<0,"too high",SUM(ABS(A2:D2)))

8   If the sum of the values in row 3 is greater than 5,000 then return the average value of the range, otherwise return the total value.

=IF(SUM(A3:D3)>5000,avg(A3:D3),SUM(A3:D3))

9   Using IF functions, test cell A4 and if the value is less than 100, multiply cell A6 by 1.01, if the value is between 101 and 200, multiply cell A6 by 1.05 and if the value is more than 200, multiply A6 by 1.10.

=IF(A4<=100,$A$6*1.01,IF(A4<=200,$A$6*1.05,$A$6*1.1))

10   Repeat question 9 using a LOOKUP function.

=$A$6*VLOOKUP(A4,$A$16:$B$18,2)

	A	B
15	Lookup Table	
16	0	1.01
17	100	1.05
18	200	1.1

Chapter Ten

1   What is the maximum number of records that can be held in an internal list?

An internal list is restricted by the number of rows in a worksheet, which is 16,384. Since an internal list needs a header row containing the field names, the maximum number of records is 16,383.

2   What is the maximum number of fields that can be stored in an internal list?

Fields are represented by columns in the worksheet and thus in an internal list the maximum number of fields is 256.

3   Are there any limits on the number of records and fields stored in external lists?

The only restrictions are those implied by the external application. Furthermore if you want to retrieve data from an external list to manipulate within Excel the above limitations apply to the amount of data you will be able to read into a worksheet.

4   What special considerations are there when entering details from a personnel register into a worksheet so that the Excel list management features can be used?

Each record in the list must be entered across a single row in the worksheet with each field in adjacent columns. Each field must have a heading which will be used when interrogating the list. Information from the personnel register needs to be divided into fields in such a way that it can be analysed as required. For example, first name, last name and middle initial may need to be entered as separate fields, as may the different parts of the address.

5   Assuming you had a list of customers which included a field showing average monthly expenditure, what is the easiest way to sort the list so that those customers spending most were listed first?

Position the mouse somewhere on the average monthly expenditure column and click on the *Sort Descending* button on the Standard toolbar.

6   Describe two ways of sorting a list on two separate fields, for example first by County and then by Postal Town?

One technique that can be used is to first sort the Postal Town field using either the *Sort Ascending* or *Sort Descending* buttons, then sort the County field using either of the *Sort* buttons.

Alternatively select **Data | Sort** and fill in the field heading for County in the *Sort By* box and the heading for Postal Town in the first *Then By* box. Click *OK* and the sort is performed.

7   How could you display those customers located in London?

Select **Data | Filter | AutoFilter** to activate AutoFilter. Click on the arrow to the right of the Location field. Click on the London option and those records will be displayed.

8   How could you display those customers located in London or Edinburgh?

With AutoFilter enabled click on the arrow to the right of the location field and select *(Custom...)*. Select London in the first box and Edinburgh in the second box and then click *OK*.

9   How could you display only those customers with an average monthly spend of £50,000 or greater?

With AutoFilter enabled click on the arrow to the right of the location field and select *(Custom...)*. Click on the arrow to the right of the *comparison operator* and select > to represent "greater than". Click in the box to the right of the comparison indicator and type **50000**. Click *OK*.

10   How could you display the expected total monthly income from those customers located in London or Sheffield?

With AutoFilter enabled click on the arrow to the right of the location field and select *(Custom...)*. Select London in the first box, click the *Or* button and select Sheffield in the second box and then click *OK*. Then select the cell in the monthly income column, beneath the last record and use the *AutoSum* tool to insert a Sum function. This will calculate the total of the values for the filtered records only.

Chapter Eleven

1   What are the limitations on the macro name?

The macro name can be no more than 46 characters long, and can contain letters, numbers and underscores, and must start with a letter. It cannot contain spaces or punctuation marks.

2   How can you tell if the name given to a macro is acceptable?

As you enter the name into the Record New Macro dialogue box, Excel will limit you to a maximum of 46 characters, but will allow you to type any combination that you want. It is only when you click the *OK* button that the name is validated, and if it is not acceptable then a dialogue box is produced to tell you so.

3   How can you delete a macro?

To delete a macro select the *Tools | Macro* commands, highlight the name of the macro to be deleted, then click the *Delete* button. You will prompted to confirm that you wish to delete the macro before it is erased.

4   How can you obtain help on a macro command or statement?

Help in Excel is context-sensitive, which means that if you select something then activate help, you will receive information on whatever was activated. Therefore to obtain help on any macro command, position the insertion point somewhere in the command and press F1.

5   If you write or record a macro into a named workbook and you save it to disk, what do you need to do if you want to run the macro the next time you start Excel?

Before the macro can be executed the workbook in which it is stored must be loaded into memory. If necessary you can automate this process by placing the workbook into the XLSTART directory so that it is loaded every time you start Excel.

6   Would you need to record or write a macro if you wanted to place a button on the Standard toolbar that inserted the current date into your worksheet?

Yes, it would be necessary to produce a macro that inserted the current date as Excel has no automatic facility for this. The procedure that would need to be recorded would be to select *Insert | Function*, choose the *Date & Time* category then click the *TODAY()* function. Alternatively the **=TODAY()** function could be typed in with the macro recorded enabled.

7   How many different keyboard shortcuts can be used for running macros in Excel?

It is potentially possible to have 26 separate keyboard shortcuts for running macros - CTRL+A to CTRL+Z. However, some of the possible combinations are already used for other things, such as CTRL+C for copying and CTRL+V for pasting, and therefore it may not be appropriate to use them.

8   Is there a limit on the number of buttons that can be placed onto a toolbar?

The number of buttons that can be placed onto a toolbar is effectively limited by the displayed size of the toolbar. If it is docked then the toolbar can only show as many buttons as will fit in the width or height of the screen. If the toolbar is floating then more buttons will be visible.

9   How do you remove a button from a toolbar?

Select *View | Toolbars | Customize*, then click and drag the button away from the toolbar to remove it completely. If you just want to move the button, then click and drag it to its new location.

10   How could you allow a user to run a macro by clicking on a chart that has been inserted into the worksheet?

Highlight the chart and select *Tools | Assign Macro*, then choose the macro you want to associate with the chart and click *OK*.

Chapter Twelve

1   How many graphic file formats can Excel recognise?

Excel can recognise up to 6 specifically named graphic file formats: Windows MetaFile (WMF), HP Graphics Language (HPGL), Computer Graphics Metafile (CGM), Encapsulated PostScript (EPS), Tag Image File Format (TIFF) and PC Paintbrush (PCX). However, depending on other applications that are installed it may be able to load other file types as well, such as BMP and RLE.

2   What command is used to insert a picture into an Excel worksheet?

To insert a picture that is held in a file on the disk, the *Insert | Picture* command is used. It is also possible to use the Clipboard, DDE or OLE techniques to insert a picture that has been generated in another Windows application.

3   How can you preview a picture prior to inserting it into a document?

Having selected the *Insert | Picture* command, the resulting dialogue box will be found to contain a *Preview Picture* option in the lower right hand corner; if this is checked then each time you click on a different picture file in the file list, the image will be previewed on-screen.

4   What is the difference between using a corner handle and a side handle when resizing a picture?

Sizing a picture using a corner handle will allow you to alter both the height and the width, whilst sizing with an edge handle stretches the picture in one direction only – either horizontally or vertically.

5   How can you maintain the aspect ratio of a picture when resizing it?

If you drag a corner handle with the SHIFT key held down then the aspect ratio (i.e. the proportions of height to width) is maintained. This is a good way to ensure that the picture still looks "right" after it has been resized.

6 How long does information remain on the Clipboard?

Information generally stays on the Clipboard until it is replaced with other information that has been cut or copied, or until you exit Windows. However you may find that due to memory constraints the Clipboard is cleared without you knowing, so you should always try to paste information as soon as you have cut or copied it.

7 What does DDE stand for and what is the benefit of using this technique?

DDE stands for Dynamic Data Exchange, and provides a way of establishing a general-purpose link between two Windows applications. Having transferred data from one application to another using DDE, this approach ensures that any changes made in the source application (the one providing the original data) are also made in the destination application (the one receiving the data).

8 When working with a DDE link, what is the difference between a *manual* and an *automatic* link?

A manual link requires that you select the *Edit | Links* command and choose the *Update* button if you want your document to reflect any changes that may have been made to the source data. An automatic link requires no such user interaction as it will ensure that any changes made to the source data are immediately reflected in the destination.

9 What does OLE stand for and how does it differ from DDE?

OLE stands for Object Linking and Embedding, and appears to offer a very similar set of features to DDE. In fact OLE can be thought of as a more elegant form of DDE, offering not only the ability to link (which works the same as for DDE) but also the ability to embed data (which creates a complete, editable copy of the information in your document).

10 How do you edit an image that has been inserted into a plan as an OLE object?

Any OLE object can be edited by double-clicking it. This causes the original application to be executed, and the OLE data to be loaded ready for changes to be made.

Index

GOVERNING FROM THE CENTRE